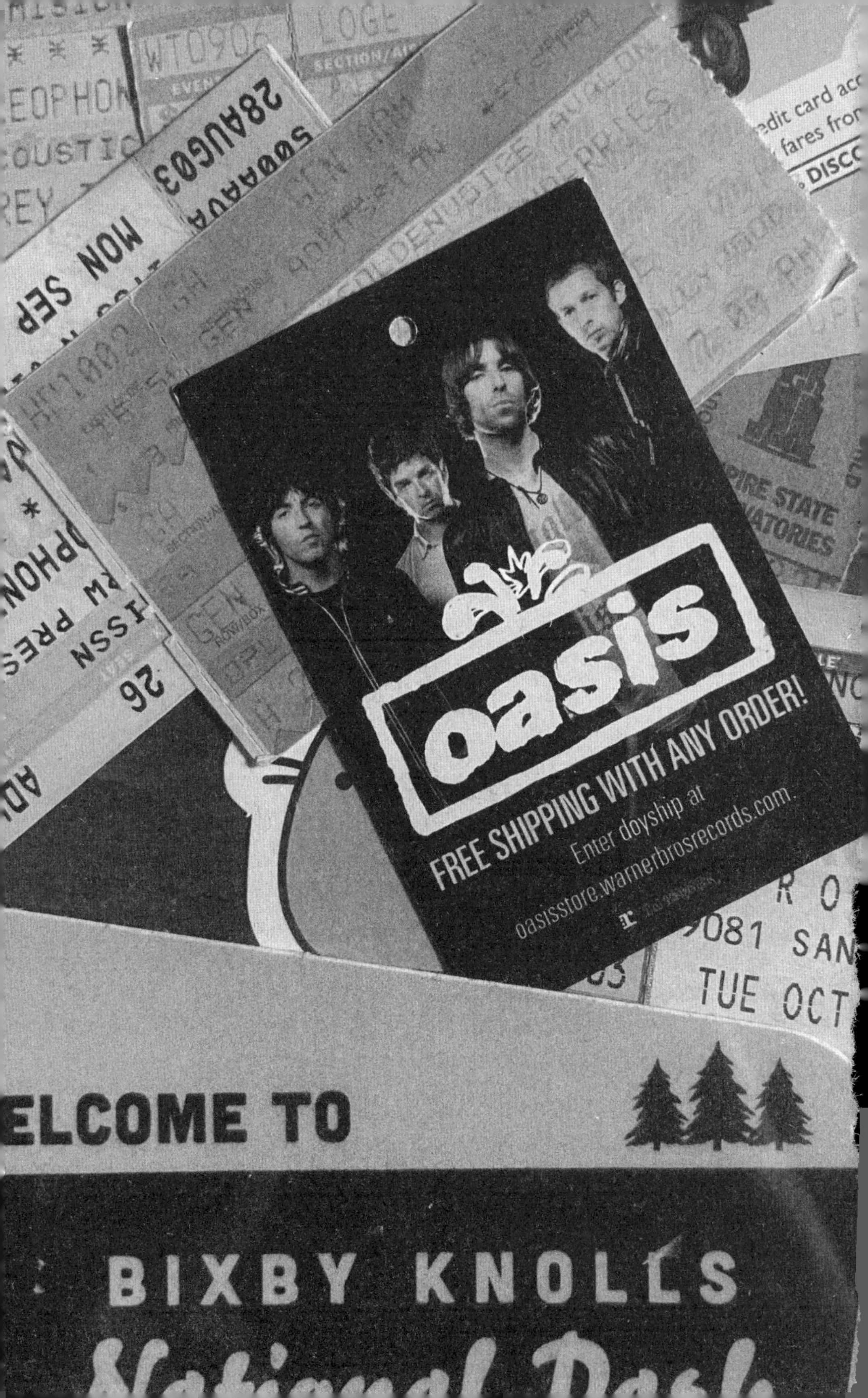
oasis
FREE SHIPPING WITH ANY ORDER!
Enter doyship at
oasisstore.warnerbrosrecords.com.
MON SEP
28AUG03
TUE OCT
ELCOME TO
BIXBY KNOLLS

AND AFTER ALL

# AND AFTER ALL

## A FAN HISTORY
## OF OASIS

---

## MELISSA LOCKER

**GALLERY BOOKS**

New York   Amsterdam/Antwerp   London
Toronto   Sydney/Melbourne   New Delhi

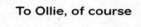

**To Ollie, of course**

# CONTENTS

## PART II:
## 1995–1998

## PART III:
## 2000–2009

## PART IV:
## THE IN-BETWEEN DAYS–PRESENT

# AUTHOR'S NOTE

The songs on that record, they're extraordinary songs, but they're not extraordinary because of anything that I did. I only wrote them, and we only played them. It's the millions of people who fucking sing them back to you since that have made them extraordinary.

—NOEL GALLAGHER IN *SUPERSONIC*

This is the story of Oasis, but probably not the one you've heard before. The story of the two brothers from Burnage who grew up in a council flat and became the biggest band in the world has been told. There are many books, countless articles, several concert films, and multiple documentaries that recount the rise of Liam and Noel Gallagher and their friends from Manchester, originally Paul "Bonehead" Arthurs on guitar, Paul "Guigsy" McGuigan on bass, and Tony McCarroll on drums. You've heard about how they stood on the shoulder of the giants of Manchester's legendary music scene, a town that birthed Joy Division, New Order, the Smiths, Happy Mondays, Inspiral Carpets, and the Stone Roses. It's well established that they quickly rose from playing the back rooms of pubs to putting on the biggest concerts in the world. They toured for years, found fans around the globe, and encountered paparazzi everywhere they went. Their songs like "Wonderwall," "Don't Look Back in Anger," and "Champagne Supernova" became anthems for a nation. The two brothers fought and fought and eventually broke up before they were supposed to take the stage in Paris. That story, which played out onstage, in recording studios, and in the greenrooms of venues around the world, is well-documented. This is the story of the fans and the folks behind the scenes and in the nosebleeds. These are the memories of the people who bought every album and B-side and T-shirt and poster and scrap of memorabilia. It's a record of the people who queued overnight to be first in line to buy tickets and albums; the folks who slept in train stations and on overnight buses to see Oasis play at Wembley or Knebworth or Palacio de los Deportes; the fans who built a community online and in line and standing shoulder to shoulder at shows. These are the fans who found kindred spirits in those working-class boys who conquered the world, and who *know* that Oasis changed their lives.

This is the story of the fans who crashed ticket-selling sites and sold out Oasis reunion shows everywhere as fans rushed to see the band once again, or for the very first time, who plan to sing back every word at a concert in River Plate or take over for Liam and Noel at the Rose Bowl, transforming the band's words from lyrics into something absolutely extraordinary. This is *their* story. These are their recollections of growing up with Oasis, falling in love with their songs and with each other, following them around on tour or only seeing them once. Because these are memories from ten, twenty, thirty years ago, not everything may be entirely factually accurate, but that's because memories rarely are. These stories come from the heart.

PART I

# EARLY DAYS — 1994

# THE EARLY DAYS

Prior to joining Oasis, Noel Gallagher reportedly auditioned to play guitar in the Manchester band the Inspiral Carpets as they were building a name for themselves. He was turned down, but then came on as their roadie, following them around the world on tour. He also answered their fan mail, which is how Gregg Weiss ended up being one of the first people in the world to know that Oasis was about to become a household name. He didn't live in Manchester, and he wasn't a music industry insider; he was a college student in Maryland.

It all started when Gregg realized he had a few questions for a band he liked and, in those pre-internet days, couldn't easily find answers. So in the early nineties, he wrote the Inspiral Carpets a letter. "I asked a bunch of questions: Are they going to come to the U.S.? Are they putting out a new album? Is there a new single coming out? And I asked the band for, like, an autographed photo, if they wouldn't mind sending one. Sure enough, three or four weeks later, a letter came back from the Inspiral Carpets, and it had their famous cow logo on the outside of the envelope. I remember pulling it out of the mailbox and walking into my dorm room to open it up. I was so excited. I opened the letter. And it was handwritten, and it was on Inspiral Carpets letterhead, too, which was super cool," he recalls. [Ed. note: Yes, the Inspiral Carpets had their own stationery.] "But the first thing I did was, I glanced down to the bottom, because I was curious who had written back. Was it the singer? Was it the keyboard player? Was it the drummer? Who was it? And I was really confused, because the letter was from a name that I wasn't familiar with. It was signed from Noel Gallagher. Was Noel Gallagher a boy? A girl? I had never heard of Noel Gallagher, but nevertheless, I read the letter, and it was really sort of cheeky. It included answers to a bunch of my questions, and I was thrilled to get something back. It turned out Noel Gallagher was the roadie for the Inspiral Carpets. So I thought it was slightly disappointing that none of the band members themselves wrote to me, but I thought it was really cool that at least someone took the time to write this kid a letter to answer his questions. So I decided to reply. I wrote back to Noel Gallagher and asked some more questions, and was kind of prying for information about the Inspiral Carpets and their next release and stuff. In what I think was my second letter, one of the questions I asked the band was what other bands are the Inspiral Carpets into. And Noel wrote back to me and answered my question and listed a bunch of bands that they were into, and amongst that list was a band I'd never heard of—Oasis." Gregg still has the letter and reads off the list of bands: the Stone Roses, Happy Mondays, the La's, the Real People, U2, Blur, Guns N' Roses, Ice-T, the Beatles, the Doors, Santana, Oasis, the KLF. Then he says, "I'm sure there's more. I'd heard of every single band in the list, except for Oasis, which I didn't even think much of. I was just like, 'All right, that's cool. Maybe that's another band for me to discover one day.' But I sort of dismissed it and didn't think about it at all until a couple years later, in maybe late 1993, early 1994, when I got wind of this band called Oasis that were supposed to be the next big thing. They were putting out their first single, 'Supersonic,' on Creation Records, and it was going to be an *NME* single of the week. So I put two and two together. I hadn't looked at that letter in a couple years, but I remembered Oasis, and I remembered Noel Gallagher, the roadie of the Inspiral Carpets, and light bulbs just went off. Thankfully, I'd saved the letters in a folder, and, I think it's a pretty one-of-a-kind piece of memorabilia. Unfortunately, the letter isn't dated, but it talks about the Inspiral Carpets preparing for the release of their next single, and they listed 'Dragging Me Down' as the single. If I remember correctly, that came out in early 1992, which dates the letter to late 1991, early 1992."

In one of the three letters Gregg exchanged with the Inspiral Carpets, Noel told him that when they toured the U.S., he should come to the stage and ask for Noel. "So I did," Gregg says. "It was at the old 9:30 Club in Washington, D.C. Capacity three hundred to four hundred, maybe, at best. And I went to the front and I was kind of shy, and I was just like, 'Hey, Noel, it's Gregg, we've written back and forth.' And he was like, 'Oh yeah, of course. It's you. Nice to meet you. I have a lot to do, but thanks for saying hi.' It was a brief exchange. There were no cell phones back then, so I don't have a photo of us together, or anything like that, but it was still sort of cool. He seemed glad that I came to say hi, and I know he remembered the letters and was genuine enough."

Thanks to his pen pal, Gregg was invested in Oasis early on. "The day that 'Supersonic' came out I was on the University of Maryland shuttle bus between classes to go to Silver Spring, Maryland, to the local record shop, Vinyl Ink, because I knew they'd have it," he recalls. "I bought it the day they got it in stock and I loved the song." Then he scooped up a copy of "Shakermaker." "I was actually kind of disappointed by it, and I tried so hard to love it the way that I loved 'Supersonic,' but I remember feeling slightly betrayed. And then the third single came out, which was 'Live Forever,' and I was like, 'All right, this is awesome. This is going to be the best band in the world for a long time.'"

———

The first time Colin White saw the band that would become Oasis, he was standing in the audience next to Noel Gallagher. "He said, 'That's my little brother on there,'" recalls Colin. "And the next thing, he joins the band, brings some of his songs in, and, yeah, the rest is history."

Colin, who now owns the record store Vinyl Revival in Manchester, grew up in that city. He was in a band, went to gigs, and spent all his free time at Manchester's infamous nightclub, the Haçienda. "It was like a church," he says. "It was something you had to go to every week."

Manchester has a long and storied musical history that doesn't fit into a few lines in a book, as it spans decades with ties to Thin Lizzy, the Fall, and the Buzzcocks, and the city played host to the Sex Pistols' first show. During the 1980s and '90s, music became the city's greatest export thanks to bands like the Smiths, Joy Division, and then New Order. Then came "Madchester," a scene built around the Haçienda and Factory Records, the independent label owned by local impresario Tony Wilson, who devoted his life to the city's music scene. The house and rave scene of the late eighties and early nineties saw the rise of the Happy Mondays, Inspiral Carpets, Stone Roses, and James, which currently is the only artist to have a plaque on the apartment complex where the nightclub once stood.

In the early nineties, anyone young and cool was making the scene, including Colin, who was running around the city's music venues with his friends when he crossed paths with the Gallagher brothers. "I grew up with Craig Gill, he was one of my best friends, and was a drummer in the Inspiral Carpets, and Noel was their roadie. That's how I got to know Noel, and then Liam was a bit younger, but he was up at Craig's quite a lot," says Colin. According to Colin, at that point in Manchester, everyone was in a band or in the music industry in some way. He was in a band called High Society, which never managed to put out an album but played around Manchester. "Because I was in a band in the early nineties, Liam used to chat to me about it. Liam told Colin that he had just joined a band, called Rain, which featured Liam along with Paul 'Bonehead' Arthurs and Tony McCarroll on drums. He told me, 'We've just done some demos 'cause we've got some free studio time for painting it.' I used to have a van with a cassette player and he said, 'Oh, come and have a listen to me demos.' And I think it was the first two tracks that were by him and Bonehead. Was it 'Alice' and 'Take Me'? It was the first-ever sort of demos put down by the band."

Noel had been playing guitar for years and was touring as a roadie with the Inspiral Carpets when reportedly he called home and his mom, Peggy, told him that his kid brother, Liam, had started a band with some friends. Noel was intrigued. So intrigued that he eventually joined the band, started writing songs, and soon the band became Oasis first in name and then in stature.

Colin liked what he heard at those early shows. "I think I went to the first four out of five gigs, first two at the Boardwalk. There were maybe thirty, forty people at the first gig at the Boardwalk," he says. He was impressed with what he saw, although he thought the sound needed some work: "They had the swagger that the Smiths had and the Stone Roses had, you know? There was a cockiness, you could call it. But obviously, gig by gig, they got better and better. And then when Noel came in and started to write the songs, it was a game changer."

After those early Oasis gigs, Colin didn't see the band again until they played Maine Road in April 1996. Needless to say there were a lot more than thirty-five people there, and he may have had a touch of regret over not auditioning for the band when he had the chance. "When they first got rid of Tony McCarroll [in 1995], because I was a drummer in a band, my name was put in the hat, and I did get a phone call saying, would I like to go and audition for the band?" he says. "And I never did, but it's probably because I thought I wasn't good enough, and the other guy who got offered was a guy called Chris Goodwin, who was a drummer in the High and was in sort of an early lineup of the Stone Roses. He was a much better drummer than me. I was a very basic drummer, so I would have never got the job anyway, but yeah, I did politely decline."

Colin's life had moved on a bit by the mid-nineties, too. He wasn't going to as many shows and was just growing up a little. Now that he runs the record shop, and spends so much time once again immersed in the Manchester music scene, telling his stories, and selling the music to the young fans who come in, he realizes how incredible it all was. "It was the norm just to think, 'Oh yeah, everyone's mates have bands and everyone goes to the Haçienda,' and it's not till years later you realize you were a part of something really special."

# KING TUT'S WAH WAH HUT,
## Glasgow, Scotland,
## May 31, 1993

Debbie Ellis is way too humble to admit that she played a pivotal role in Oasis history. She is the reason the band was at a gig where they were seen by manager Alan McGee and then signed to Creation Records.

Debbie Turner, as she was known at the time, was in a band called Sister Lovers, who shared a practice room with Oasis. Debbie and her bandmate Lorraine Hayward knew Noel from around town and because they also lived in Burnage, where the Gallaghers had grown up. Debbie and Lorraine met when they were both working at Affleck's, a sort of DIY department store that is still selling clothes, accessories, music posters, and more to the cooler kids in Manchester. They were early hustlers and started a sound engineering course, a band, and got jobs at a local pub, too. "That's how we met Liam," recalls Lorraine. "He came in one night to the pub with a few mates. I think we were sort of pulling his leg a bit because he had, like, a kind of sixties bob haircut." Lorraine and Debbie quickly hit it off with the group of guys. "Because we lived in Burnage I think we said,

'Come back to our house,' because we lived around the corner from his mum, and just sort of from that time, we all sort of became sort of mates." It was sort of meant to be, anyway, as Manchester was a small town and they already knew Noel and Mark Coyle, who became the soundman for Oasis, and they all hung out at the Haçienda and the bars on Oldham Street.

When Debbie and Lorraine started their band, Liam suggested they share a practice space and the cost of rent for that room. Their room was in the Boardwalk, an old redbrick Victorian schoolhouse that had practice spaces and a small venue for bands to play. "They'd rehearse, and then we'd wait for them to finish, and we'd go in," Debbie recalls. Sharing a space meant arguing over the decorating. "Oasis used to put a Union Jack up," Debbie says. "We found it a bit offensive at the time because it was the early nineties, and we were a bit like, 'That looks like National Front, like a right-wing thing.' And obviously they were doing it because they were into the Who and the sort of British Invasion bands or whatever. But still, we used to go in and rip it down every time we were in, and then the next time it'd be put back up. So then what they did was they painted a Union Jack—badly—on the wall." When Debbie's friend, Creation Records' Alan McGee, came up to Manchester to see one of his bands play at the Boardwalk, he ended up in the practice room that Sister Lovers and Oasis shared. He asked, "Who is this band?" inquiring about the Union Jack decor. "So I said, 'Oh, they're called Oasis.' And he went, 'What are they like, an Oi! band? You know, like right wing?' And I just went, 'Yeah . . . ' But I was just pissing about."

Debbie, who is now a photographer, had a front-row seat to the band's musical evolution, too. "They sounded a lot different early on.

They really changed, evolved as a band. I suppose it was Noel writing the songs, because I don't think he'd been in the band that long when we moved into the room. So the songs were changing over time. Early on, it was, like, these seven-minute songs with, like, a five-minute guitar solo and Liam singing a bit like Ian Brown [from the Stone Roses]. He hadn't really found his voice. And I think Noel's love of U2, you could hear that," she says. "By the time they played in Glasgow, they'd got a demo tape together. They'd recorded in Liverpool with the Real People, and you know that they'd sort of helped them create their sound. It was more concise, more hooks. The way Liam sang was really coming together. He found his own voice, so to speak. Over two years, or eighteen months, their sound really changed." Debbie and Lorraine went up to Middleton to watch Oasis play one of their early gigs. "They were on support for [New Order bass player] Peter Hook's band Revenge," she remembers. "They were quite polished. The only gripe me and Lorraine had was that Liam was just standing there, he wasn't moving enough, which is funny now."

Sister Lovers, Debbie's almost all-girl band ("we had one guy," she notes), had been rehearsing a lot, too, and hustling to get a gig. They finally managed to snag one at a small club in Glasgow, Scotland, called King Tut's Wah Wah Hut and she was very excited, because back then it was a challenge to get an out-of-town show. "Around that time, in the nineties, it was pretty hard to get gigs outside of Manchester, so the only place you could really play was the Boardwalk, where the rehearsal room was, and they had a venue upstairs. So you could get a gig there, or at the local pub in your area, or something like that. It's not like now how you can email a promoter and say, 'Oh, this is my band, listen to my demo, and watch my YouTube video,'" she recalls. She couldn't wait to tell her friends about the show. "For us to get a gig in Glasgow, it was quite a special thing. So I went into the practice room while we were swapping over, and Noel was putting his guitar away, and I just sort of burst in and was dead excited about this gig—and quite cocky as well—saying, 'We're playing in Glasgow, so there!' That kind of thing," she says. "I don't know what possessed me, but I think he might have given me a dirty look. He looked up from putting his guitar away, and it must have been like a knee-jerk reaction for me to sort of go, 'Oh, why don't you do it? Like, I'm not being mean, I'm just sort of happy for all of us, so why don't you do it, too?' Then he sort of just ran with that and they ended up coming up to the gig, even though they weren't booked on to play at that show in Glasgow."

Debbie didn't mind the band tagging along. "Nothing really fazed me," she says, laughing. "We were both just bands trying to play our music. It wasn't a case of 'Oh, go and do a gig and get signed.' Nobody thought like that. It was just the experience you were doing it for. Just the experience of getting in the back of a transit van, traveling two hundred miles, and playing at a very small venue on a Sunday or Monday night."

Both bands rolled up to the show in Glasgow, but there was one problem: Oasis wasn't on the line-up, the venue wasn't expecting another band to turn up, and didn't really want them to play an already packed bill. Oasis and the friends who had come along to the gig rolled into King Tut's to hear the promoter tell them a resounding, "No way." "There was about twelve of them all together in this part that was set off from the stage, and they were all crowded in there," says Debbie. "And the promoter said that they couldn't play because they weren't booked. So the legend goes that they threatened to smash the club up, which they didn't. I don't remember that. What happened was all the bands in solidarity with Oasis said, 'If they're not playing, we're not playing. So you've not got a gig, you've got no one playing.' So, yeah, they got to play four songs."

The show at King Tut's was Sister Lovers' first gig and Debbie's old friend Alan McGee wanted to support her, she says. "It was because I'd been friends with him for quite a long time, and he found out that my band was playing there, and he was just like, 'Oh, I'll just go along to that and freak her out and stand in the audience and just stare at her,' you know? That's his sense of humor." It was Alan who helped convince the promoter to let Oasis play, according to Debbie, noting that *not* letting them play was more hassle than it was worth. So Oasis took the stage and Debbie was impressed. "They had done a few gigs—I'd seen them play in Middleton and at the Boardwalk—so they'd got a lot more polished. It was my first gig, so we were quite shambolic, whereas they were a lot more polished."

Debbie wasn't *that* impressed, though. "We shared the room and we chatted to them. It's like a family member or something," she says. "Even when Alan said he's signing them, it's like, 'Well, Alan signed loads of bands and they'd never been like this massive global success.'"

When Oasis released their debut, *Definitely Maybe*, on Creation Records, Debbie went to take a listen. "I went to HMV, and they used to have these listening booths in there, and I listened to it from the first side through to the second side and I was quite blown away," she says. "I just thought the energy had really been captured on the whole album." She didn't buy the album, though.

"I saw Liam in Warrington at the Stone Roses gig when they reformed, and I shouted out to him, and he was like, 'Oh, hello,' and he was asking me if I still did music, and he's really friendly. And he said to me, 'The check's in the post, Debbie,'" she recalls, laughing. "So I'm still waiting for my check."

———

Johnny Hopkins was in bed when his phone started ringing. And ringing. And ringing. In the middle of the night. "It rang and rang and rang and I thought, 'Oh my God, what's happened? Has someone died?' I thought, 'I better go and pick it up,'" says Johnny. "I pick it up and hear 'Johnny, it's Alan.'" Alan McGee was his boss at Creation Records. "I said, 'Yes I can tell it's you, but look, it's midnight and I'm in bed with my girlfriend. Can we talk tomorrow?' He said, 'No. I've just seen this really amazing band. And I'm going to sign them and you're going to do the press' and blah blah blah. I said, 'Okay, Alan, it's really late, and I'm in bed with my girlfriend, can we not just talk tomorrow?' And he said, 'They're brilliant. They're, like, the songs of the Beatles, but delivered by the Sex Pistols or something.' I said, 'That sounds really brilliant, but I just want to go back to bed.' And he says, 'All right, all right, we'll talk in the morning.' I put the phone down, got back in bed."

It was a short-lived peace. "About half an hour later, the phone goes again. It's Alan with the same spiel, but magnified a little bit more. He was even more excited, and he was embellishing the story as it went along, saying the band had threatened to trash the venue unless they were allowed to play," recalls Johnny. "I'm getting more and more interested in the idea, even though it's really kind of bedtime for me. I was like, 'All right, Alan, I get it, I'm glad you want me to do the press, but let's talk in the morning.' Literally, every half an hour, throughout the night, he kept calling me, and he got more animated and more excited. Not sure why it got more animated and excited, I can make a guess, but I'm not going to. By about half one I was completely sold on the band. By half six in the morning, I was really fired up and ready to do the job, but a little bit tired."

Alan McGee got back to the London office the following day and handed Johnny a cassette. "It was the kind of famous live demonstration tape that had about ten songs on it, most of which ended up on the first album," he explains. "The thing about this demo cassette was it had a properly designed cover. Most demo cassettes in those days came with, like, handwritten lists of tracks and a contact number, no kind of design as such. This cassette had the name of the band superimposed over the Union Jack going down a plughole, or going down the toilet. So it's sort of like a sort of psychedelicized, distorted Union Jack, and I thought, 'God, that's a really clever image. It seems to be saying something political about the state of the U.K. after fourteen years of Tory government.'" The wheels started turning in Johnny's head, thinking of the press opportunities that working with a band like this could create.

# THE BOARDWALK,
## Manchester,
## July 3, 1993

A few weeks after listening to their demo cassette, Johnny Hopkins and a few of his music-minded friends went up to the Boardwalk in Manchester to see Oasis live for the first time. "We all had our jaws stuck to the floor in utter wonderment and awe at just how good they were," Johnny says. "I'd seen bands that had record deals and albums out that were a million times worse."

After the gig, Johnny hung out with the band, and at one point went over to Noel's apartment, which was just around the corner. "The answering machine was flashing, so Noel pushes the button to listen to the message. The voice comes through and it's another Mancunian voice, saying, 'Hi, it's Johnny. I thought the gig was amazing.'" It was Johnny Marr from the Smiths. "If you got to choose a famous fan to start things off, Johnny Marr is a pretty good one," he says. "Of course, they accumulated loads of celebrity fans like Lars Ulrich from Metallica and Evan Dando [of the Lemonheads] and all these people, but Johnny Marr is just the coolest, basically."

Johnny Hopkins, although likely Marr as well, was getting more and more excited about Oasis. "There's certain ingredients that you want in a group early on to determine how successful they can be," he says. "You want good songs. You want them to be great live. You want them to be great in interviews and have something to say, you want them to look good, and you want them to generate interesting stories. They were ticking every box that a PR person wants." Oasis had it all, and even more important, "They had ten quality songs, all of which pretty much could have been singles," he said. "It was mind-blowing."

# ARENA AMSTERDAM, The Netherlands, February 18, 1994

Now that they were signed to Creation Records, Alan McGee had big plans for Oasis. First was getting them out of the U.K. for their first international gig. To make that a reality, he got them a spot opening for the Verve in Amsterdam. The Verve was blowing up at that point and it was a very good opportunity for Oasis to start making a name for themselves internationally, because while they were building a little buzz in the U.K. on the strength of their live shows, no one anywhere else had any idea who they were. All they had to do was take a ferry over and play. Instead, a fight broke out on the boat, most of the band was arrested, the gig was canceled, and Creation Records' publicist, Johnny Hopkins, had to figure out what to say to the press.

"Everyone was excited about them at that point, so to get a supporting stop with the Verve was a really valuable thing from an awareness point of view," says Johnny. "I decided to do some photos in Amsterdam because I really wanted to distinguish them. Differentiate them from all the British groups of that particular time who were very, very much stressing their Englishness or their Britishness. I thought that was a really dangerous cul-de-sac to go down, and I really didn't want the band to be seen in that light because I felt that there was so much more about them. They were a band that could stand on their own two feet and didn't need to be part of a movement, you know? And besides that, they were all basically Irish Mancunians, so they were several steps away from most of the other musicians who ended up under the umbrella of Britpop. So I thought, 'Well, they are playing in Amsterdam, so let's go and do a photo session in Amsterdam, which will show already that this is not your average English band.' Plus, it looked cool that they were playing a gig abroad with the Verve before they even had a record out."

The band headed over on the ferry, but Johnny and a photographer flew in a short time later and headed to the hotel. "It was little more than a boardinghouse, really, and there was no reception area," Johnny recalls. "It was just like a 1950s telephone table that you have in a house just there in the middle of the hallway. I thought, 'Oh god, this is a bit grotty,' but you know, whatever. We stood there for a few minutes and sort of shouted out, and a woman came down, who obviously worked at the hotel. We said we're meeting this band from England called Oasis and she says, 'Ah, yes, you better call their room.'" Johnny had no idea what was going on. "No one had mobile phones. Everything was a surprise, sometimes a good one, sometimes a bad one," he says. So he called the hotel room and Noel picked up the phone. "He told me I better come up, but don't bring the photographer." A bad surprise it was, then. Johnny headed up to the room, which was dormitory style, meaning everyone should have been sleeping in the same room. However, when Johnny got up there only two people were there: Noel and the sound engineer, Mark Coyle. "I'm thinking, 'Where's everyone else gone?'" he says. "Where are the other four members of the band and the other road crew and their mates from Manchester who were going out there selling merch?" Noel told him to sit down. "I'm like, 'What can be so bad that he wants me to sit down and listen to what he's got to say?' So obviously, something bad has happened," Johnny says. Noel explains that they got into some fight and had been put into the hold of the ship. While Noel seemed to be expecting Johnny to panic, he had the opposite reaction. "I think the way that Noel told it, they were put in cells, locked in cells, or something," remembers Johnny. "Could be true, could be embellished. It didn't matter. The story was *so* good, I just willed it to be true. It was delivered with such panache and humor that you just wanted it to be true. And I knew that the press would want it to be true in all its detail."

Johnny starts thinking through the situation: "So on the one hand this is a really great rock and roll story. On the other, I was going, 'Shit, we've come out here, spent quite a bit of money on planes and the photographer's time, and we haven't got a photo shoot because the guys had been kept on that boat and sent straight back to England. And also they've not had the experience of supporting the Verve and playing abroad and all of this.'"

Johnny realizes that this ideal rock and roll story will really have an impact only if he can get a photograph. "There's obviously no photograph of the fight, because people weren't carrying around mobile phones and documenting everything, and the band aren't here, but Noel's here." Johnny decides he needs to snap a photo of Noel, but there was one problem: "He was so pissed off, understandably, that the gig had been blown, that he really didn't want to have his photo taken," says Johnny. "I think his feeling was that the band had blown it a little bit. One of the things he did when he joined the band was draw some order into them and make them practice hard and make it more professional. So blowing their first gig abroad didn't really go down very well with him." After some explaining and coaxing, Johnny managed to persuade Noel to have his photo taken. "I found a very distinctively Amsterdam bridge over one of the canals where there was a lamppost that happened to have a poster for the gig that named not only the Verve but also Oasis. That meant nothing to anybody in England, and certainly meant even less to anyone in Amsterdam, but it had their name on it. I just said, 'Noel, please just pose there with that poster for like a minute, we'll get a shot, and that will go with the story. We'll get a lead news story in the *NME* next week,' which we did."

Later, the brothers squabbled about the ferry incident among other contentious points during a now-infamous interview with *NME* journalist John Harris. The resulting insult-laden audio was released in 1995 as "Whibbling Rivalry" under the name Oas*s. The fourteen-minute single ended up on the charts, reaching number 52 on the U.K. Singles Chart, and *Pitchfork* dubbed it "easily one of the best Oasis records." The boat story and Johnny's spin on it went far in creating the Oasis mythos and he wanted to build that reputation up even more. While Oasis didn't get to open for the Verve that time, they got something arguably better—a legend. That buzz paired with their electric sound helped establish them as the next great rock and roll band. Johnny knew that as a publicist he would need stories to give out to different publications and that the band was a gold mine, so he had an idea. "Going back to the first time I met them, and the first few nights out in Manchester that I had with them, it was very, very clear that they were the kind of people around which stuff just happened, you know? Interesting stuff, mad stuff, funny stuff, so very early on I said to Noel, 'If anything interesting happens, phone me up and tell me, and I'll write it down in a little black book, and we'll stick it out there when we need a story,'" Johnny explains.

Johnny knew that some of the stories were clearly true, while others were based on truth but slightly embellished, and some were probably made up. "But they were so engaging and sort of believable, we decided we'll run with them, and the press will print them, because there's such great stories." So some of the stories about, say, Oasis nicking a golf cart at Gleneagles and going for a joyride may not be entirely true, but it's utterly believable at the same time. "I mean, if it was Coldplay, you might go, 'Oh, well, it's not true.' But with Oasis, you would believe it was true," says Johnny.

"So that started a series of calls—probably two or three times a day—telling me these amazing stories," he says. "And I've still got the books locked away in a bank vault. All the notebooks with all the stories in them."

# THE ANGEL,
## Bedford, U.K.,
## March 23, 1994

Neil Primett was twenty-five and booking a small club in Bedford when he had an idea. "So round about end of '93, going into '94, I would always do in January what we call the Tips for the Year. The music press did it in London, and I wanted to replicate the idea in Bedford. So it was, like, try and put on as many bands that were up-and-coming," he says. "The only problem with that is the bands wouldn't have had a hit record and they're not particularly big, so you are running the risk of a poor turnout, but you just want the credibility of it. Because I had a Saturday night in a small town, we had something of a loyal following—we put acts on, and I'd have a DJ, so people would turn up to enjoy a band and then stay late for the music."

Neil was working on his January Tips for the Year programming when he got a cassette of a new band from a booking agent. "So Ben Winchester, the agent, sent me a demo tape round about November 1993 of Oasis and one of my DJs got sent a DJ vinyl. I'm gonna forget the name of his DJ vinyl, but it was something that was never

released, and I got this five-track demo, which I've still got to this day,"
he explains. "I've got these tracks on the cassette. I'll be honest, rightly
or wrongly, I wanted to get as many people out as I could, so I loaned
the cassette to a few people. I had a young pal that was a student in
sixth form college, whether that means anything to you, they're like
seventeen- or eighteen-year-olds. He'd play the music in a common
room, where there's plenty of people, so people like him were helping
me get the word out, because Oasis were relatively unknown at the
time. I was keen to do the show in January and Ben originally agreed
to a show in January. I even created the poster for the January show,
only to be called by Ben saying the show's off. He couldn't string
enough dates together for Oasis at the time, so he was just going to
do a one-off show in London at the Water Rats and try and generate
some press, and then go with a full tour late March, April, with the
'Supersonic' single."

While Neil was disappointed, he booked Oasis to play the club on
March 23, when they were starting a co-headlining tour with Whiteout, a Scottish band also on the rise. It was the first day of the new
tour and Oasis was slated to release their first single, "Supersonic,"
on April 11. "Honestly, the first date of the tour is not the best day
because the profile builds, momentum builds, everything builds the
more airplay the music gets," says Neil. Luckily, he had done what
he calls something "naughty" and given the cassette to the teenagers,
who then turned up to the gig. "I remember Oasis were confused that
the people in the audience were singing the words, because they knew
there's no way anyone could be singing the words. I had five songs on
this cassette, and they must have played seven, and watched people
singing five of them. And I bet you all the keen ones were down in

the front from this school. I think Liam did cop people singing the words."

Despite Neil's efforts to ensure a packed house and burgeoning fans, the turnout was sparse at best. "I mean, we had about a hundred people, and I'll be honest, that was the worst turnout I'd had. Definitely the worst turnout at the time," says Neil.

Neil wasn't exaggerating. Lorraine Hayward of the Sister Lovers had gone with her cousin to see her friends play at the Angel and they were unimpressed. "I told my cousin, 'Oh, this band we share a room with? They're playing near you, Bedford, you want to go?'" Lorraine recalls. "I said, 'I'm going to gig a lift down. Do you want to come and meet me?' And Laura, my cousin, I was talking to her about this the other day, and she was like, 'Right, it was in this pub miles away from anywhere and there was no one in it.' She was like, 'Oh my god, I remember seeing them and there were like four people in the room!' I think they were there as tour support, so that was part of it, but still."

According to Neil, the folks who were there weren't necessarily that impressed with the band, or at least its lead singer. "The night they played, they got a sort of arrogant swagger," he says. "We hadn't seen a band before where the singer looked like he couldn't be bothered. And I think for some people, they didn't take to it. Most fans that had turned up, the singer had performed, but he was just hanging off the mic, appearing to make no effort, you know, which has become his trademark, but at the time, confused some of my audience, if you know what I mean, because it was the first time they'd seen him."

Luckily he hadn't paid the band a lot of money. "They played for one hundred pounds, they were not big fish at all. So a hundred pounds was certainly not a lot," he says. "We charge three pounds fifty in advance, four pounds on the door, and I must have gone a year without losing money on any show. I think they were one of them rare shows where I probably lost money."

Neil was intrigued, though, and went to see Oasis perform again. "We'd go and follow them and see them at other shows, and I'd got a clothes shop selling retro trainers, which I have now, 80s Casual Classics, but at the time, that was my thing, retro clothing, and Oasis saw the trainers we were all wearing, and were like, 'Where'd you get them? Where'd you get them?' So we paid a visit to one of the gigs with a box of trainers and sold them a whole load. And we must have done that on three occasions. So that sort of relationship continued," he says.

While the show didn't work out the way he hoped it would, it has paid off in other ways. After all, being able to say that Oasis played at his little club gave him a certain cachet and, eventually, the ultimate compliment: people claiming they were there when they weren't. "Too many people have been claiming they were there," he says. "And in years later, I'd say, 'Did you ever go on a Wednesday night?' Because a lot of these people were regular on Saturday, but it's quite a big deal to go somewhere on a Wednesday if you've got to get up the next day."

———

While the show at the Angel had been small, it was kicking off something much larger: a co-headlining tour between Oasis and White-out, a harmony-driven Scottish rock band trying to make a name for themselves, too. The tour came about thanks in part to the band's manager, Andrew McDermid, or McD. While now he is a university lecturer, at the time he was a bold Scottish band manager who had no qualms about interrupting conversations. "Liam and Guigsy were standing at the bar in the Hop & Grape in Manchester, and I walked up to them. All I remember saying is 'I am McD, I manage Whiteout, and we got a record deal.' And Liam replied, 'Well, so have we,' in the sort of puffing-his-chest-up kind of way. But as a result of that conversation, we ended up agreeing to do some gigs together. And that is kind of where the Oasis and Whiteout connection comes from—a conversation in a bar in Manchester in October, which culminated in a tour in 1994. So the first Oasis headline tour was actually a co-headline tour with Whiteout, for better or worse."

Eric Lindsay of Whiteout was on board with the plan, because he had already met Oasis and discussed the same thing. Whiteout had come down from Scotland to Manchester for a show and also for a Heavenly Recordings showcase at the Haçienda. "In attendance that night were members of Sister Lovers, including Debbie Thomas, who is now Debbie Ellis," Eric says. "Her and our bass player hit it off and she was very good friends with Oasis, obviously. So we met, either there or the night before, I can't remember, but some of the guys were there and it was at that point I think that Guigsy said to me, 'Let's do our tour together.'"

Eric went to go see Oasis play for the first time at the Cathouse in Glasgow, where they were supporting the Verve. "I went along and kind of went upstairs backstage afterwards and then kind of hung out and everything," he says. "At the Haçienda gig, the gig in Manchester, as a band, we were discussing doing the co-headlining tour."

The two bands became friends, or friendly enough that when Oasis had something to celebrate, they headed to a Whiteout gig.

"The day that Oasis signed their recording contract, Whiteout were playing at the Camden Falcon in London, and they came along to the gig having just signed a deal, and Bonehead asked if they could go up and do a song before Whiteout went offstage," remembers McD. "So we said yeah, and they went up and did 'Shakermaker' minus Noel, who stayed at the bar."

When Whiteout was booked to play on *The Word*, a Friday night television show that would later host the TV debut of Oasis (and Nirvana's international TV debut of "Smells Like Teen Spirit"), Liam was in the audience to check out the band. "Oasis played about two weeks after that and we were just kind of bumping into each other at various things at this point. And then management organized the tour, so we did the co-headline tour," Eric recalls. "So we had met them quite a few times before we went on tour together."

According to McD, the tour was supposed to be three weeks long, but ended up being only sixteen dates, and it all kicked off at the Angel. For his part, McD was curious to see Oasis in action. "Although we got on really well with them, I was still the manager of their competitors, if you like," he says. "We're on tour together, so I was kind of thinking, 'Right, what's the competition here?' So they went onstage and it was the first time I'd seen them onstage as a band from the audience properly and I thought, 'Right, singer looks cool. They can sing. Guitarist looks a bit like Al Pacino.'"

His overall impression of the band was: they had potential. "They were memorable," he says. "Everyone tells me in hindsight they knew Oasis were going to be huge, but that's nonsense, just hindsight. I was there at the time thinking, 'Will they be huge? Have they got potential?' And in the context of the U.K. music industry at that time, I thought they were a good band. I would say that over the time period that I got to know them and their behavior, I would say that they had tenacity, that you could have seen it coming."

As the tour progressed, it was clear that something was, in fact, coming. "We played our first gig in Bedford, I think it was a fifty-fifty split audience of people there to see us, people there to see them," remembers Eric. "Tour lasted about a month, and as the tour progressed, it was pretty clear that they were definitely attracting more people than us."

However, fans wouldn't have necessarily known, because White-out looked like the bigger band from the outside of the venue. "We had a tour bus, because we had good tour support from our label, Silvertone Records," Eric recalls. "We would roll up to every gig in all these tiny little venues, in the tour bus, and Oasis would turn up in a transit van with Bonehead driving it, having slept in some skanky bed-and-breakfast the night before. There was good banter about how we were the pretend rock stars and they were keeping it real for the working classes. And we were all working-class kids with a more or less similar mindset."

The two bands played up and down the U.K. and then made a memorable stop at the 100 Club in London. "The 100 Club was a massive gig as well. Obviously, just for the history of the Sex Pistols and what have you," says Eric. "And I am pretty sure Liam got a bottle thrown at him that night. My best memory of him that night was kind of showing his true colors, of being just a really up-for-it, positive character. He was just talking to everybody, and it was like you could just tell the whole thing was in front of him at that point, and he was totally excited by the whole thing." The show was reviewed by

*NME*, who dedicated a few lines to Whiteout, but gave Oasis the title of Best Live Band in the Country. It's hard to compete with that.

The last gig the bands played together was at the Duchess of York in Leeds. "By that time, there were queues way down the street," Eric recalls. "And I think for the last maybe three gigs, they just head-lined. There was some wangling about the co-headline, but the last few nights, they headlined, and there was queues way down the street that night, and they weren't to see us."

The tour ended and Oasis went on to sell out stadiums and top the charts, while Whiteout continued on a smaller scale and slower pace. "It was a bit bittersweet, because it was a brilliant experience, it was great to see things growing exponentially in those weeks," says Eric. "It was just unfortunate that the majority of that growth was for them."

The two bands played together one more time, at T in the Park in Glasgow in the summer of '94. "We were maybe like fourth on the billing. I can't remember if they headlined that or what, but we saw them again and had a kickabout backstage and a laugh and every-thing," recalls Eric. "We kind of met up a few times, but obviously our careers went on different trajectories."

For McD's part, there's only one real regret he has about that tour: "The leg of the tour in Scotland was a wee bit disjointed because we're from Greenock, and we'd originally spoken about Oasis playing there and doing that together, and I actually said, 'No, we can't, because Whiteout don't want to do their hometown again until they're bigger.' I must have kicked myself a million times for that, because I could have been the guy who booked Oasis to play in my hometown, but I didn't."

# THE JUG OF ALE,
## Birmingham, U.K.,
## March 28, 1994

As Oasis and Whiteout continued their U.K. tour, they came to Birmingham to play a little pub called the Jug of Ale. Arthur Tapp, a longtime promoter at the Catapult Club, was working at the Jug of Ale at the time, but didn't think he actually promoted the show. "Only real memories I have are of Ocean Colour Scene (who were regulars at the venue) asking who Oasis were when the posters went up in late 1993." Ocean Colour Scene were at the show and soon met the band and ended up touring with them for years.

"Whiteout told us, 'We're playing Birmingham, at the Jug of Ale, do you know it?' We went, 'Yeah, that's our local,' and they said come along and watch the support band, it's called Oasis," Iain Huddy remembers. Iain was friends with the Ocean Colour Scene crew and ended up working as their tour manager for years. "Oasis was the support band, and halfway through the tour, they became the headliners. That's how good they were."

The Jug of Ale, Ocean Colour Scene's local in the Moseley area of Birmingham, was just around the corner from where they were living at the time. "It was like the local music pub that had DJs in the week, and upstairs, bands would play. It was only like a hundred to a hundred and fifty capacity in that little room," says Iain. "From there you would play the Birmingham Irish Center, which was about five hundred capacity, and then you go up to another level, et cetera, at Edwards. Oasis played Edwards and we saw them there as well."

There were only thirty or forty people in the room when Oasis played the Jug of Ale's small stage, but Iain says the response was instantaneous. "You knew in thirty seconds," he says. "Within one minute of them starting, it was just like, 'What the fuck is this?' Everyone in that room knew straightaway. It was just the noise, the sound, and Liam, well, Liam was Liam. As soon as you saw him, it was like, 'Oh, well, he's a rock star and they're gonna be fucking huge.'"

Ocean Colour Scene and Oasis ended up hitting it off that day in the pub. "After the show, there was no real backstage area, so we kind of went along and said hello and realized we had mutual friends in a band from Liverpool called the Real People, who Oasis had been doing their demos with," Iain says. "Ocean Colour Scene and Oasis hit up a friendship and they ended up going on two tours with them." They played together throughout the 1990s and 2000s at gigs like Newcastle, Irvine Beach, Sheffield Arena, and Knebworth—and they kept playing together until Ocean Colour Scene played the V Festival at Weston Park in 2009, but Oasis failed to take the stage. They broke up a week later.

As he toured with Ocean Colour Scene, Iain had a front-row seat to Oasis's rapid rise in fame. What started as two bands on tour, playing shows, suddenly became something else. "It changed so quickly when Oasis started to get famous, the paparazzi started being around the whole time. It just became this whole other thing," says Iain. "I remember coming out of my hotel room in the morning to go down for breakfast, and as I came out the door, a photographer took some photos. He'd been hiding down the end of the corridor hoping to catch a snap of one of them, and he heard a door opening, and took his chance. It was like, 'Fuck me. This is ridiculous. This is the hotel corridor!' To go from playing in a pub to having photographers hanging out in hotel corridors—to having that level of attention—in the space of twelve months was just insane."

# DUCHESS OF YORK,
## Leeds, U.K.,
## April 12, 1994

When Ian Dowson rolled into the Duchess of York in April 1994, he was not there to see Oasis. "We went to see the band who were supporting because we quite liked them, a band called Whiteout," he says. "The story was that Oasis had played there the year before, in '93, and no one turned up. It was literally the owner of the pub watching, and that was it. But this was packed out." That said, it was a pretty small club, capacity 250 or so, that Ian describes as a place "for bands on their way up"—and Oasis certainly was that.

While he was there for Whiteout he stuck around to see Oasis, too. "It wasn't the greatest gig, I've got to admit," he says. "Because it was in Leeds and they were from Manchester. There was quite a bit of rivalry between the two towns. There's not too much distance between us, so it's a bit of a rivalry. And at one point, I thought Liam was going to get lynched, just with the attitude he had coming on, you know? Not giving a shit and just being a bit arrogant. But it went down well, and it was packed out, you know? You could tell the hype was kind of starting."

Ian didn't walk out of the show as a fan of the band. That came the next time, when he saw Oasis play at the Leeds Irish Center, a slightly bigger venue for a band who still hadn't released their debut album. "We knew a bit more of their material by then. The album hadn't come out yet, but I think 'Shakermaker,' the second single, was just out," Ian says. "It was just amazing. They played 'Shakermaker' to begin with, which was sort of mid-tempo, but then they played 'Fade Away,' which was quite a fast rocker, and the place went mad. Pints flying everywhere. It was brilliant. Didn't play for long, maybe fifty minutes, didn't do an encore. They finished with 'I Am the Walrus.' It was one of those gigs where everyone's just coming out of the place drenched in sweat. People were like, 'Wow, what was that?' That was a turning point."

After that show, Ian was firmly a fan. So he went to see them at Middlesbrough Town Hall in the winter of 1994. "It was still only music fans who knew about them," Ian recalls. "There wasn't amazing hype as such, but that was a great gig. I just remember coming back buzzing over the actual gig." Ian liked what he saw onstage and the energy coming out of the music, so he kept going back. He went to see Oasis play Sheffield Arena, the band's first arena gig, and then went to Earls Court, Maine Road, and Loch Lomond. It was a big change from seeing them in sweaty pubs in Leeds. "Yeah, two years later, I was watching them at Knebworth," Ian says. "Normally, other bands, I wouldn't have probably been that bothered, but with Oasis it was like we just got taken along for the ride. It was like our little gang."

Ian kept going and going to gigs. "The following year, when *Be Here Now* came out, people were clamoring for tickets. They were that big and successful then that it was really hard getting tickets. But we got tickets in Exeter and Newcastle, which were like two extremes to the country. We were in the middle, and we have to go two hours up north or six hours down south," he remembers. "That was the last time we saw them."

After ten shows, Ian realized he had watched the band grow until they outgrew him, and were too big and too popular for him to enjoy, particularly after seeing them perform in such small venues. He wasn't tempted by the reunion gigs in 2025, either. It's not that he doesn't still love the songs, though. "The songs and the songwriting have a universal feel," he says. "You can go into a bar on a weekend at the end of the night, and if 'Don't Look Back in Anger' comes on everyone in there is singing it. And how incredible that everyone knows that song, just three minutes of music that brings people together."

# WETLANDS PRESERVE,
## New York City,
## July 21, 1994

While Oasis was slowly building a reputation in the U.K., in the U.S. only the most ardent Britpop fans with an eye on *New Music Express* and *Melody Maker* and an ear on import releases knew about them. Despite early signs of success in the U.K. with growing album sales and increasing crowd sizes, to really be a smash hit, the band's record label knew they needed to crack the States and the U.S. market, so the label sent them to New York City to play for a small crowd. Three hundred people flooded into Wetlands on a steamy night in July to see Oasis play as part of the New Music Seminar, a music industry convention that brought folks from all over the world to check out the musical rising stars. The band still hadn't released their first album, but their two singles were starting to attract attention.

Another band that was invited to play the seminar was the Julies. "Oasis came out as we were sort of hitting our stride. They had hit theirs, and we were fans," says Chris Newkirk, who still plays with the Julies. "I also DJed at a place called the Melody Bar in New Brunswick [New Jersey]. I didn't DJ regularly, but I was friends with this guy named Matt Pinfield, who was a radio DJ at the New Jersey indie rock station. And he would invite bands over, like, we DJed with two guys from Radiohead. I got to DJ with lots of sundry bands that I had their records, et cetera. Matt was a very early adopter to all things breaking, as he has been known to be, so he started spinning Oasis from the very first single the day or week it came out. So there was a host of people already dancing and getting into that band in Central New Jersey."

So the Julies, or at least Chris, knew of Oasis before they met them at a New Music Seminar event held at Webster Hall in New York City. "We went to this opening-night party, and Echobelly, if you know them, performed. They're a Britpop band. We just ended up backstage, it was kind of a party, but not a party. It was just people hanging out. They had several bands play, and everybody was playing three- to five-song sets as a sort of showcase. Backstage, a couple of us from my band were hanging out with Echobelly and other people I can't remember, and Oasis shows up, and we're hanging out. That was my first introduction personally to them. We were just all backstage, hanging out. And, you know, Liam was sort of walking up and down the stairs, Webster Hall has like seven sets of stairs everywhere, and. I just kept running into Liam," Chris says. "You know, it's so funny, because the persona that we all see today is probably as much as his true persona as anything. But there was a side of him that was like this chill guy, even though it was probably his first time in New York, or first time in New York with the red carpet, and he was just chill as can be. Even at that stage, he was just, like, a really chill communicator and really not what we were reading in the press. In the press you're reading about them destroying hotel rooms, but they were chill as can be."

Since Oasis wasn't performing at Webster Hall, they invited everyone they met backstage to come see their set at the Wetlands. "We made plans to meet up there with Echobelly to watch," says Chris. "Wetlands is a small space, and there was, like, the small floor, and then there's this little ledge in the back. It's not a balcony. It's just like a one big step up, I think. And I remember standing up there with Andy [Henderson] from Echobelly and watching the first-ever Oasis show [in the U.S.]. They gave out free T-shirts. I know they're a stadium or arena band these days, but back then, it just seemed to really suit them to play that size venue. And with Liam's sort of personality, with his hands crossed behind his back and his head cocked to the left or the right to deliver all his vocals, it was just perfect at a place like the Wetlands. I know it translates in an arena, too, but it just felt like, in a New York City rock club, it was perfect."

Jerry Rubino, a longtime radio promoter, had a slightly different take. "To this day, I think Wetlands is the weirdest club ever. You walk in, and it wasn't like the stage was in the back, it was like, sideways. I remember Liam going into the second song and actually saying, 'Turn it up. Turn it up!' because he probably couldn't hear himself, because it was, like, twenty-five feet between the stage and the back wall." Jerry fell in love with the band, who he has since seen at every show they've played in New York and New Jersey. "I remember Liam just comes out and says, 'Hello, New York, "Shakermaker,"' and that was it!"

One of the people crushed into the dingy space was Ken Weinstein, who is the president of Big Hassle Media, a music publicity company, but at the time he was working as a publicist at Atlantic Records. He was there with two friends, both music journalists.

"Those two guys, as much as you could do so in America, they were on the streets of England," says Ken. "They were aware of every seven-inch, every single, every new anything that was coming out at the time, so as Oasis was starting to ripple in the U.K., we were buying their early singles. I fully got turned on to those guys by them, and so they were coming over to America to play at Wetlands for New Music Seminar. I was not part of the scene that was going to Wetlands at the time. It was a curious place for them to perform at, because it was sort of a post–Grateful Dead scene, like I think I saw like the Zen Tricksters there."

Despite the odd choice in venue, the show was packed, which was impressive considering *Definitely Maybe* wasn't even out yet. "I think just like the 'Supersonic' single and maybe 'Columbia' were out at the time, but, man, were they fucking awesome," Ken says. However, he didn't walk away from the show with a bigger love of the band. In fact, he kind of hated their performance. "We were pissed off at that show. That show offended me," he says. "My favorite rock stars like the Who, the Clash, they were fucking adamantly into it, and were not removed emotionally onstage at all. I was not prepared for Liam's sort of high-and-mighty holier-than-thou, kind of dismissive-of-the-audience attitude, essentially. I wasn't ready for that attitude of his. The attitude eventually became his trademark, but when first taken in without warning it was a lot. Because, remember, in those days, there were no videos, no YouTube. I mean, they sounded amazing, the songs were fucking amazing, and his voice was incredible. Everything about that part was just like, 'Holy shit, this sounds so good,' but he was such a dick in my head, like he didn't give a shit about us. It was almost like he was in a room without us, and there was no emotion.

He wasn't getting into the music. There was no dancing. There was no head banging. It was like delivering the lyrics and delivering the vocals—really well—mind you, like fucking singing his ass off, but without almost any obvious sense of connection to it, like no emotion. So that was really off-putting for me and my pals at the time. I thought it was incredible, but I was not ready for the Oasis attitude. But then, you know, when the album came out, I was like, 'Okay, I love this thing.' Literally, a perfect album."

Ken went and saw them again and again and again. He was hooked. "By the time I go to see them at Roseland [in October 1995], I'm ready for it. I'm fucking loving it," he says. "It was just such a sing-along at that point. And the best part of seeing Oasis became literally shout-singing, top-lunging, every lyric with the band and everyone in the audience."

———

Also in the audience that day was Michael Howe, who had come up from Philadelphia to see Oasis on their first U.S. outing. Like Ken and undoubtedly almost everyone in that packed room, Mike really liked British music. You had to be low-key obsessed to know about Oasis in the U.S. at that point in their career, back in the days before the internet was widely available to the general listening public. "I was part of a group of friends who were super Anglophiles, and we would read NME and Melody Maker and Select on a sort of a religious basis. And one of us, somebody, bought the 'Supersonic' single just as it was issued, and we kind of fell in love with that and just became sort of devotees from that moment onward."

Like all good religious devotees, Mike and his friends decided to take a pilgrimage, this time to New York for the band's first show. "Three or four of us went up to Wetlands and saw the show, and we're just kind of smitten," he says. "The place was small. I think the capacity was probably two hundred and seventy-five or three hundred. It was very crowded. I don't remember offhand who else was on the bill that night, and I'm not sure that we arrived in time to see anybody else. All I remember seeing that night was Oasis. I was standing right in the middle of the floor, probably ten feet from the stage. There's actually a photo of me and my friend Brandon Schmidt in the crowd that was in, I don't know, Paolo Hewitt's book, or Paul Mathur's book, one of the early, early Oasis books. And, you know, we basically stayed there for the whole show. I shouted out something like 'Way to go, Bonehead!' in the middle of the set, and he kind of looked surprised. It was an impressive show. Impressions were made. I can tell you that much."

The next time Mike saw them was when his band opened for them at JC Dobbs in Philadelphia.

# RIVERSIDE,
## Newcastle, U.K.,
## August 9, 1994

Steve Spithray was intrigued by the music coming over the stereo at a house party in Durham. Someone's parents were away and the teenagers had taken over the house and, of course, the stereo. "I just remember thinking it sounded a lot different to anything else that was around at the time," he says. "I just remember thinking, 'I need to hear more of this band.'"

It was the white-label demo version of "Columbia" that had been recorded by Oasis, and someone at the party had gotten their hands on a copy. Steve liked what he heard, so when he saw that they were playing in a nearby town, he got a ticket. "We went to see them in the gig they did at the arena in Middlesbrough," says Steve. "Happened to be the day that Kurt Cobain died. I think it's been quite well-documented that Liam dedicated 'Live Forever' to him on the night. I can't give you a huge amount of information about that concert, I'm afraid, because I was quite drunk, but it was very busy. Even by that point all the gigs were selling out in, like, no time. That was early April '94, so that would have still been prior to 'Supersonic' being released.

"They were an absolutely ferocious live band in those early days. And I was going to, like, a lot of gigs of different genres of music at the time. They were just so much better than everybody else in that kind of heavier indie guitar sound that they were doing," he says. "It doesn't make any sense, because they just stood there and none of them did anything."

As someone who went to a lot of gigs, Steve noticed something different about the band and the crowd they attracted. "There was always something underneath the surface with them, the feeling that something could potentially go wrong. Even at that point you could tell that Noel and Liam weren't always agreeing with each other or seeing eye to eye all the time, so there was always that, like, little bit of sense of danger, and that's a bit of a cliché, but there was always that to it," he says. "And I think that spilled over into the fans that were attending. Not only were they all sold-out gigs, but even by, like, mid-'94 there were people going to the gigs who weren't normal, like, gig-goers. It was already starting to spill over into the football terraces. So when people that go to football suddenly start wanting to go and see gigs, it's kind of crossed over. And they were already doing that really quite early on. So that added a bit of extra to it."

For anyone raised in the era of Taylor Swift's Eras Tour or even head banging at a Metallica concert with your devil's horns in the air, it may be hard to imagine going to a concert and fearing your fellow audience members. However, the mid-nineties were a different time. "Maybe it was some of the sorts of gigs that I went to, but there were gigs around that time that were quite intimidating in terms of being the audience," Steve says. "And I would say Oasis were probably one of the worst for that. Oasis were always a lad band, so they always attracted that laddie, sort of cocky, boozy attitude."

That tension bubbled to the surface one night in Newcastle at a small club called Riverside. "Newcastle Riverside was about a six-hundred-capacity space. The ceiling was about eight foot high, so you could almost bang your head on it if you were jumping up and down. Sometimes it got so hot that sweat would be dripping from the ceiling," Steve remembers. "It's one of those proper old basement venues."

Steve and his friend had tickets to the show, but they were with two other friends who were hoping to buy some from a tout, or ticket scalper. "We got chatting to a tout outside, and he said, 'I haven't got any tickets, but I'm getting some in a bit,'" Steve recalls. "And then Noel Gallagher jumps out of this taxi, walks up to the tout, pulls out, like, a roll of paper tickets, and gave them all to this tout. And then the tout starts selling them for, like, three times the ticket price." While there is no way of knowing if that was really Noel, Steve guesses that the guy was Noel's mate and had been doing it to make some extra cash, and apocryphal or not, it could explain how the show became so crowded. "It was one of those gigs that you never get anymore, that had just been massively oversold," says Steve. "It was so busy, I can remember having, like, a pint in the entrance to the men's toilets, just because that was the only place we could find to stand."

They enjoyed listening to the supporting act, Ocean Colour Scene ("Even at that stage they were touring with good lineups"), but everyone was there to see Oasis. "The first song they played was 'Listen Up,' and it had never been heard before. It was a brand-new song, and the place just went absolutely wild," he recalls. "And that was for a song that had never been heard by anyone before."

The show moved along with perhaps more banter than usual, as this was Newcastle United territory and because they knew Oasis were Manchester City fans, there were football chants coming from the crowd.

"I can't remember exactly what was said, but there was just back-and-forth, and about the fourth or fifth song—it was 'Bring It on Down'—and I remember seeing out the corner of my eye, Noel jumped offstage. I don't think I actually saw the guy get onstage and punch him, but Noel went in the audience. Then I remember seeing Liam, like, literally going headfirst in the audience after Noel," Steve recollects. "And then it all kicked off to our right. I think they were all in the audience, apart from the drummer, and then they just went offstage. I wasn't kicking off in the venue at that time, but then Liam came back onstage about two minutes later. Everyone was going nuts again, but he wasn't coming back onstage, he was just basically saying the gig's over and piss off home. Like, 'Nobody jumps on our stage.' And then it did start getting a bit, like, nasty."

The audience poured outside the venue and Steve recalls seeing skirmishes in the street as fans opted to fight each other over the canceled gig, but then the amped-up and aggrieved fans remembered who they were really mad at. "The venue had a stage door sort of around the corner, so that's where their van was," Steve says. "I remember suddenly everyone went around the side, which is where they come out the venue. And by the time we got there, the van was being, like, shaken and stuff. Everyone was just starting to get quite nasty by that point. I mean, if anybody had broken into the van with the band inside, I don't know what would have happened."

That experience didn't turn Steve off the band, though. He followed them closely for years. Yet no show was quite as memorable as that Newcastle gig.

———

Also at the show was Henry Smith, who similarly had fallen for Oasis thanks to the early singles and was eager to see them play live and maybe even meet the band. He had gone to Volume Records and picked up a ticket. "It's a handwritten ticket, which they were in those days," he recalls. "It cost, I think, five pounds."

Tickets in hand, Henry and his friends left school early and headed to the venue. "Me and my mates had worked out that if you went to the venue about three o'clock, the band would come in and do a sound check," he says. "We used to hang around, and we always used to get into the venue to watch the sound checks and meet the bands. And we did that with Oasis, and they were lovely. They were absolutely lovely. They let us in, let us watch the sound check, and just chatted away to us a bit. They were really friendly. And I had a signed T-shirt that got lost somewhere in the house. They would kick us out, to clear the venue out of people, and then open the venue formally. And I remember it being really busy. Like, I think they'd sold probably a third more tickets than the capacity. It was absolutely rammed. Even right at the back, it was rammed."

Despite the packed house, Henry and his friends elbowed their way through to have a good view of the show. "We were right at the front when the band started. Like, right there, because there was no barrier—just the stage and then the band. Then this guy climbed over my shoulder and punched Noel in the face about halfway through the gig," Henry recalls. "He threw a right hook to his eye, and the band went off. Liam came out and just sort of hurled up abuse on us, 'You can't do that!' Newcastle is kind of a tough, working-class town, and Oasis at the time, they had a lot of kind of bravado about being tough working-class lads. Eventually the lights came on and we realized they're not coming back on and there was a sort of sense in the crowd, like, 'What? They're not coming on because of that? It wasn't that big a punch. He's not that badly hurt.' And there was quite a bit of anger in the crowd.

"Gigs were raucous events back then, and it wasn't unusual for someone to get onstage and maybe stage dive, that happened all the time, but there was a kind of unspoken rule that you don't get involved with the band. You don't stop the music," he says. "So the guy who threw the punch got dragged out by the bouncers, and people were hurling punches at him as he was being dragged away."

Since the music had been stopped, Henry had no choice but to leave the venue. "I remember we went outside, they were offering us half-price tickets to a terrible band called Kinky Machine, terrible like sub–Manic Street Preachers copy. They were awful. And the anger really blew up outside. The ambulance came to collect Noel, and there was a certain attitude, like, you didn't need an ambulance for *that*. Soft, that's what they were saying. And people were throwing glasses at the ambulance. So it was getting a bit nasty. The gig had been live on Radio One at the time, too. And the *NME* described it as a riot outside. It wasn't a riot. That's exaggerating things, but there was a lot of anger towards them, a sense of, you know, 'You're all talk, you're not as tough as you say, why don't you come back out?' I've no idea why this guy did this. Just probably got carried away and was drunk."

On his way out the door, Henry did grab a souvenir: "I got the set list from that gig onstage," he says. "I managed to grab it. It's kind of torn a little bit at the bottom. There's a reissue of *Definitely Maybe* that's just come out, and the set list on the inside of it is exactly the same as mine. *Exactly* the same. I'm almost beginning to think they may have gotten a photo of mine from when I put it on Facebook years ago, because it's exactly the same, even the tear is in the same place."

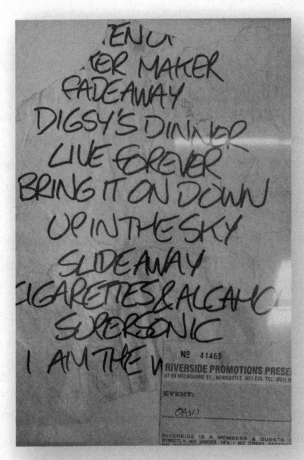

Iain Huddy has a slightly different perspective on the gig. He had been working and touring with Ocean Colour Scene and was in the unlucky position of being on the wrong side of the not-quite riot. "I was stood at the side of the stage with Oscar [Harrison], the drummer from Ocean Colour Scene, and a guy who worked with Ocean Colour Scene called Bertie [Dunn]," Iain recalls. "It all kicked off at the front of the stage and we—the three of us—piled in to kind of rescue, because I think Liam jumped in the crowd. It's all a bit fuzzy. But we ended up pulling people out of the crowd, because it just turned to chaos. Then we all just went backstage into this tiny little dressing room. So in this tiny little dressing room, literally ten meters from the stage, was the whole of Oasis, the whole of Ocean Colour Scene, and outside were all these Newcastle people banging on the door to get into the dressing room. We had to barricade the door! And then Oasis had a car pull up, and they just left. They left! And off they went and we were kind of . . . fuck. We were stuck in this room with all these mad Geordies just going mental. And then we had to get our gear and load up the van while people were lobbing bricks at it. Oscar and Bertie stood out by the van with baseball bats. It was absolute carnage. And it was all live on Radio One."

The tour had to go on, though, so the next night both bands reconvened at the next venue. "We played at Leeds Irish Center, and everyone was like, 'What the fuck?'" remembers Iain. "Everyone caught up with each other and it was almost like a real camaraderie was made between the two bands then. Because they knew what happened, they knew that we'd been helping out, and we drug people off. We all just wanted to know what the fuck was that about."

# SATYRICON,
## Portland, Oregon,
## September 24, 1994

Thanks to their relentless touring and buzzy new single "Live Forever," by the time *Definitely Maybe* was released on August 29, 1994, it became the bestselling debut album ever in the U.K. (though that title was eventually passed to the Arctic Monkeys). However, Oasis was still trying to make a name for themselves in America. To that end, they were playing a string of tiny clubs down the West Coast of the U.S. Their bus rolled into Portland's Old Town and parked in front of the grungy yet beloved club Satyricon. As with most of this first tour, the band opted to hire local acts to open for them. In Portland that responsibility fell to Lincoln Brigade, who had been making a name for themselves around the music scene particularly after they were signed to Island Records.

"We were seeing the name Oasis in *New Music Express*, the British magazines, and I followed music magazines. We'd heard snippets and the stories of them not getting along even at that early stage. How there was sort of a contentious relationship between the two brothers," says Shalen Parker of Lincoln Brigade. "I heard 'Supersonic,' one of those early singles, too."

So Lincoln Brigade knew who Oasis was when they were asked to open for them. "We were approached by Ben, who was the sound guy and de facto helped to run Satyricon at that time. He called us and said, 'Hey, they're looking for a third opener.' I don't know what happened, but we ended up playing right before Oasis, but we'd played there before, and he knew us and he thought we would fit in," Shalen says.

They showed up to the gig and realized that Oasis had filled the very tiny stage with equipment and they would have to play around it, making the stage even smaller. "I had to play sort of walking down the stairs to the greenroom," says Shalen. "When I was performing, I had the mic stand on the railing so that I could sing from the stairs, so that was fun and agile."

During their downtime, Shalen and Noel hung out in the greenroom while Noel tried to convince him to sell him a guitar. Oasis had just done a string of packed-house gigs in Tokyo, Osaka, and Nagoya, and apparently Noel had developed a taste for Japanese guitars. "He wanted to buy a guitar of mine, but it wasn't mine to sell. It was a Yamaha Japanese Jaguar copy from the early seventies, '69 or something like that," he says. "And then while we were talking, Liam came in and checked in on him. He did not speak a word, pulled his round glasses down, looked me up and down and seemed very unimpressed, and then left."

When Oasis toured Japan, the shows were mobbed and fans surrounded them at hotels and venues. Word may have been spreading among the Asian community in the States, too. "It was packed, and I think about a third to half of the people that attended were Asian Americans, mostly Japanese women," Sha-

len recalls. "The rest was the standard Portland crowd of alt-rock, indie rock, flannel people."

When the show started, it became clear why the band had so much extra equipment. "When they came on, it was perfect, because they had extra-loud equipment, and Satyricon had a great sound when things are very loud in there and there's a crowd," says Shalen. "Everybody came out almost hesitantly. Noel took his guitar up, and then Liam came on, and he had a big bottle of beer. He just sort of swallowed the microphone when he sang, it was incredibly impressive. He was really leaning out over the front audience, because, once again, they don't have a very big stage, so he was really right on top of you in many ways. They just put on a pretty powerful first performance."

The performance and the band made such an impression on Shalen that he wrote a song about them. "It's called 'Lightbulb Changer,'" he explains. The song can be heard on Lincoln Brigade's album *Static Electric*. "I think what they were asking onstage is, 'You want to be like me?' He was saying, 'You may not even know it, but I'm living the life that you could only aspire to.' There was a lot of pride in being a superstar and that's what I took away from that show and that's what the song's about—and also seeing myself from where I was at the time. Just in a different place and trying to make up the difference."

# BOTTOM OF THE HILL,
## San Francisco,
## September 26, 1994

Aaron Axelsen had a plan: he was going to take Blur to an Oasis show. The band was making their way down the West Coast, and as it happened so were Blur and Pulp—and they were all going to be in San Francisco at the same time. It was a bold plan because the media had been building up a rivalry between the bands as Blur's *Parklife* rose through the charts and *Definitely Maybe* made waves. The war of Britpop, as it was billed by the press, pitted the posher Blur against the working-class Oasis and generated plenty of headlines. So Aaron's plan was a deviously good one.

"I was working at this ma-and-pa record store, an indie store in Berkeley called Mod Lang Records. And Mod Lang was kind of the epicenter of British indie imports music, because the owners were from England, so we would get these imports *fresh*," he says. "So I used to order a bunch of imports and I read the *NME*, and was really into Britpop. I bought Oasis's first single, 'Supersonic,' as an import and started playing it on my college radio station in the East Bay. I was also interning at Live 105, so I brought the import to the music director before me, Steve Masters, and he started playing it. So this is even before it was serviced by Epic Records. And yeah, I think Live 105 was the first station—commercial station—in America, to play Oasis." [Ed. note: The first radio station to play Oasis in the U.S. is a matter that is up for debate. "We started playing it probably the week it came out in the U.K., so if someone was able to get it before that, well, there you go," Aaron says.]

Aaron had been working hard to introduce the people of San Francisco to the wonders of Britpop. "It was an electrifying time for music," he recalls. He was very aware when three of the bands he loved rolled into town at once. "So the night before Oasis made their debut at Bottom of the Hill, it was September of '94, the night before at the Fillmore, Blur headlined and Pulp opened." In addition to working at his college radio station and interning at Live 105, which is one of the oldest alternative rock stations in the country, Aaron was also interning at SPK Records, which was part of EMI. As part of his job, he had to drive visiting bands as they ran through San Francisco. "I would take them to record stores or, you know, to do radio interviews or press," he explains. That day, he was responsible for taking Blur around while they were in town. "Turned out my best friend at the time, Adrian Moreira, who worked for Epic or Sony, he was going to be driving Oasis around in his beat-up station wagon and taking them to do promos and stuff." Together with Aaron's boss at Live 105, they hatched a plan. "This was kind of at the beginning of the Oasis-versus-Blur rivalry. I mean, it was all kind of sensationalized by the British tabloids. They've never been in the same room together, you know? Never in the same studio together. And the cover of *NME* is touting that this is, like, the next Rolling Stones versus Beatles and all this crazy stuff. We plotted it out where we would have both bands in a studio together on Live 105, unbeknownst to each other," Aaron says, laughing. "We set this up without anyone really knowing what we were doing.

"So my boy Adrian brought Oasis, Noel and Liam, to the station first, and I went to the Phoenix Hotel and picked up Blur in my piece-of-crap 1981 Volkswagen Jetta. I drove to the station, and I remember walking into the studio and Damon [Albarn] just glaring at me, like, 'What did you do, Aaron?' Because there's Oasis," Aaron recalls. "It ended up being this really kind of magical evening where you had these two very special up-and-coming British bands, both kind of carrying different flags. Britpop kind of belonged to Blur, and Oasis was kind of the Brit rock band, and they were in the studio together for an hour on Live 105, taking phone calls, playing music. There's photos; if you google that, it's all over the place. Someone actually made, like, a seven-inch picture disc of the interview. It's pretty cool. They were together for the hour in the studio, and to this day, it's the only time they'd ever both been in a radio studio together." Despite all the press about the rivalry between the two bands, the tone of the interview was friendly, affable, and funny as the members chatted.

"And then afterwards, I took Blur with me in my car to Bottom of the Hill, so they were in attendance while Oasis played their first-ever show in San Francisco," Aaron says. To give you an idea of what this looked like, Bottom of the Hill is an iconic San Francisco music venue that is also very intimate. "They had built the stage on risers, so the stage is basically on the floor, almost like seeing a band in a garage or something," Aaron explains, but despite the garage-like feel, Bottom of the Hill was *the* destination for seeing new bands. So it made sense that Oasis was playing there and that Blur was there to witness the new band's ascension. Anyone else who crammed into that tiny room may have had no idea that they were knocking shoulders with and trying to squeeze past British rock royalty when Aaron walked in to the club with Blur and at least one member of Pulp. "Jarvis [Cocker] came, too. I got him on the list," Aaron says. "It was just kind of funny. Like, in the back of the room I'm standing there with Alex [James], and I remember Graham [Coxon] was drinking a lot, so Damon had to take him home during the show. And it was just kind of me, Jarvis, and Alex hanging out. I remember Brian Jonestown Massacre opened the show, and it was just electric. It was just one of those moments where it *felt* like a significant moment in rock history. It *felt* like the cusp of this newest wave of music was about to hit, and it just felt important and exciting. And for those who were able to get in that small little room to witness music history it was a pretty magical night."

The show that came next on the tour was also memorable for anyone in the audience, but for very different reasons.

# WHISKY A GO GO,
## Los Angeles,
## September 29, 1994

Bernadette Gilbey didn't have a ticket when she showed up to the Whiskey a Go Go, the notorious music venue in West Hollywood. She wasn't worried, though. "If you're twenty, dumb, and fearless, you can get in anywhere you want," she says, laughing. "We were students and into the Britpop scene and we also had no money for shows, so we would blag our way into every show that we could." She and her friends would find the manager or someone associated with the band and convince them to get them into the gig for free.

This was going to be her first time seeing Oasis, and despite not having a ticket or even the money to buy a ticket, she was pretty sure she would get in. "We knew the band just from being in London that summer and hanging around with them," Bernadette says.

Bernadette was being young and free in London when she found herself in a little bar in the Camden area. "We were talking to someone that we didn't realize was Liam Gallagher, and we asked him if he wanted to go dance to 'Shakermaker' with us," she laughs, thinking back. She was a devoted *NME* reader, but hadn't actually heard the music before, because the songs weren't exactly in heavy rotation on U.S. radio at the time. That was why they had no idea that the Oasis they had read about was the band that was playing over the stereo at the bar, so they asked the lead singer to come and dance to it. "And he's like, 'I can't. I can't.' And we're just like, 'Why?' And he's, 'I can't. I just can't.' And we're like, 'Okay,'" she explains. "And so we just got another round of drinks with him and then we realized, 'Okay, we're idiots, this is his song.' We hadn't put the two together at that point because we were only twenty and dumb. We were just talking to a guy with a thick accent and we didn't realize. It was a rather embarrassing time, but also, Camden was an exciting time to be twenty and American."

By the time Bernadette and her friends left London, they were fairly well acquainted with the band, so when they rolled up to the Whisky they were pretty confident they could get into the show. "We didn't find them during sound check, but we found Noel walking in and we said, 'Noel!' He's like, 'I know you.' And we're like, 'You do know us!' And then we said we don't have tickets and he just grabbed our hand and took us backstage and led us into the venue with them when they were walking in for their set time. There was this little door on the side that we went out and came down from the stage into the crowd." She was in—and about to witness one of the most infamous shows in Oasis history.

Bernadette walked to the side of the venue to watch the show. "It was really crowded. It was a sold-out show and then some. They packed as many people as they could in that night, and we were nowhere near the front of the stage," she says. It was from that slight distance that they watched everything unfold. "There was definitely an excitement built up in the room for this show. Obviously it's a room full of friends as well, because the Britpop scene in L.A. was tight-knit and so you knew nearly everyone in that room or at least had some connection to them. But everyone was very excited to see this band who was obviously breaking pretty big. They had done a radio interview a couple days before [at Live 105] and we were all amped for it," Bernadette says. "So the energy was really high, the preshow music was good, and then they came onstage and it seemed that . . . We just thought they were drunk. And they started, and I believe they started on the wrong song, or it didn't seem like the band was together, but they got it together. It didn't start off as tragic as it ended up, but I don't think it was a whole set. We were just watching them stumble and yell and fight with each other. And the crowd was just increasingly growing out of it. It was definitely an interesting introduction to seeing Oasis play live."

According to the 2016 documentary *Supersonic*, the band had been given speed instead of cocaine before the show. "I don't know who fuckin' got it, but it was there," Liam Gallagher says in the movie. "And we all thought it was coke. We were doing big fuckin' lines of it." They had been touring for months, were exhausted, and then amped up on the wrong drug. They were jittery, edgy, and keen to fight. Then there was supposedly a mix-up where a roadie gave Noel the wrong set list and the band members were all playing different songs. They stopped the gig and started over, but tensions were so high that at one point Liam threw a tambourine at Noel, who then split, not just from the gig, but from the city entirely. The managers eventually tracked Noel down in San Francisco. It nearly broke up the band and resulted in a string of canceled shows across the United States. The tour eventually resumed on October 14 at the Uptown Bar in Minneapolis.

The show hadn't soured Bernadette on the band, though. She liked the music and the people she had met in London, so she gave them another chance when they came back to town. "They came back just like a few months later and played the Palace, and it was night and day," she says. "I think that first show burned a lot of people, saying, 'Oh, they're not really worth it,' but when they came to play the Palace in the spring, we're, 'Okay, no, this band is definitely the band we thought we were going to see.'"

The shows turned her into a lifelong fan. "I've probably been to sixty Oasis shows, and of the solo shows, maybe another twenty," she says. It helps that Noel remembers her and frequently brought her backstage and she had a permanent guest list thing with the band. "Even now if there is like a little signing line, Noel will come to me first," she says. "And I'm like, 'Do you remember who I am?' And he does."

**Bernadette Gilbey and Noel Gallagher**

———

Le-Van De Guzman was also at the show at the Whisky. He had fallen in love with Britpop and British music like the Smiths and Stone Roses while he was still living in the Philippines. When he moved to Los Angeles in 1988 his interest grew. "I started listening to KROQ. I got to learn more bands," he says. It was while listening to KROQ sometime in 1994 that he heard a DJ mention a band called Oasis. "It was just a mention, though," Le-Van says. "I didn't even hear any of their songs. And then that same month, maybe May 1994, I bought this British magazine called *Select*, and it had a free cassette. The free tape was a compilation, and it had the song 'Fade Away,' the demo version of it, by Oasis. So when I saw it, I was like, 'Okay, there's Oasis.' So I got it, and then listened to it, and I just fell in love with the band. It was just pure, straight-up rock and roll."

When he spotted a newspaper calendar listing for an upcoming show at the Whisky, he was in. "I saw the ad saying Oasis on September 29, 1994. I knew I had to go get tickets for this concert," he reads off the clipping, which he still has. "The picture on it was actually crap, they're missing one member!" He walked over to a Ticketmaster location and picked up a ticket. "No lines because, back then, when they went on sale, they didn't really sell out on the same day, even though it was a small club. It was, like, probably a three-hundred-, four-hundred-capacity club, but it wasn't sold out yet," he says. "But then by the time show concert they came, it was already probably sold out. It was packed."

Le-Van got to the show early and went inside. "Every time I go to shows, especially for all these new bands, usually I would bring in a recorder. I love recording shows. I love taping and bootlegs, but for some reason that day, I didn't even bring a camera, because usually at the Whisky a Go Go, security was really tight. They would, like, frisk you and pat you all the way, so I didn't even bother bringing in a camera or a recorder. I just went in, and even though usually I like going to shows early, it was already kind of packed when I got in. I stood somewhere on the right-hand side." He stood there to watch the opening band, Pink Noise Test, and then Oasis came on.

"They started with 'Rock 'n' Roll Star,' but they had, like, a technical issue. They had to stop, and then they restarted it again," Le-Van says. [See above: it wasn't technical difficulties, it was meth and a set list mix-up.] The KROQ DJ who had first introduced Le-Van to the band was acting as emcee and the crowd was going nuts. "They were wild and there was a lot of pogoing happening, they were jumping up and down. I was doing that, too, but I was kind of really paying attention to their performance," Le-Van says. It was then that he noticed what has become Oasis's trademark stage routine—not really moving onstage. "It was funny, because my first impression was they kind of just stand there onstage," Le-Van says. "They play good rock and roll music, but they don't really move a lot. They just, like, stood there. But the thing is, I don't know. I just loved it, especially with Liam, he just stood there. He would just look at the crowd and just pretty much do nothing. He would go to the microphone for singing and then, if it's not time to sing, he just kind of backed up."

From his spot in the crowd amid the pogoing masses, Le-Van noticed things weren't exactly friendly onstage. "The thing is, you could see some sort of tension," he says. "They would look at each other, like Noel and Liam would say something. I couldn't understand what they were saying because they had all this crazy Manchester British accent, but you could tell that they were kind of saying something to each other. It was just weird. Then sometimes Noel Gallagher would look at the crowd and say something, kind of taunt the crowd, or maybe somebody from the crowd would taunt them or something. There was that interaction between them and the audience."

One thing Le-Van does not remember, though, is any tambourine throwing. He's not even 100 percent convinced it actually happened. "I don't think so. I don't," he says. "There was some sort of tension between them, but at that time, when I was watching it, it wasn't really a big deal. You know what I mean? I mean, they finished the whole thing. The whole show was finished and done until the last song. Weeks after the show, that's when I found out that they had some sort of altercation." However, when he and a few other fans waited outside the venue for an hour to see if Noel and Liam would come out, they saw only Liam. "At that time, I didn't have any clue on what happened backstage," he recounts. "I don't know why a lot of people would say that it was a bad show, but the show was pretty,

pretty, pretty good, except for that first mishap. I mean, from start to finish, it was an awesome show, and that's probably one reason why I became a big fan of them. They didn't do a lot of crazy antics onstage, they would just stand there and play, but it was mesmerizing."

As it had for Bernadette, the show cemented Le-Van's love of the band, and he's gone on to see them eleven times. He has amassed a small collection of photos and memorabilia over the years. "I would always, like, hang outside and wait for the band members, to get autographs and all that," he says. He also snuck into the back of the Universal Amphitheater in L.A. during a leg of the *Be Here Now* tour in 1998, and while evading security guards, managed to get a photo with Liam. He returned the next night and spotted Liam in the crowd watching the opening act.

"I saw their first L.A. show and saw their last L.A. show," he says. He, of course, will be at the Rose Bowl to see the band reunited. He is also crossing off a bucket list item and seeing them play their first reunion show in Manchester.

# JC DOBBS,
## Philadelphia,
## October 23, 1994

Oasis was still slowly trying to break into America by playing a string of gigs at tiny clubs. The tour was briefly interrupted after the dustup in Hollywood when Noel split for San Francisco and dates across the Southern U.S. from San Diego to Springfield were canceled. The tour restarted in Minneapolis and then headed for the East Coast, including a stop at JC Dobbs in Philadelphia.

"We were based in Philly, and our band had played JC Dobbs several times," says Michael Howe, at the time a member of a band called Propellor. He was part of the group of Anglophile friends who heard "Supersonic" more or less right when it came out and gone up to New York to see their first-ever U.S. show at Wetlands and wanted to try to nab a spot opening for them at their debut show in Philadelphia. "I had a pretty good working relationship with a woman named Kathy James, who was the talent buyer at JC Dobbs. And as soon as the dates were announced, I seem to recall calling Kathy or actually going over there and saying, 'Look, if the band doesn't have support on this date, I'd like to raise my hand for it.' So she gave us the slot, and she gave the first slot to a band called Emily's Prize, who were also friends of ours. So it was kind of a love-fest on the stage at that point."

Jason Snell, the frontman of the band, had been a fan of Oasis since nabbing the free cassette that came with *Select* magazine with the demo version of "Fade Away" on it. He hadn't been able to go see them play in New York for their first U.S. gig, though, and while he was excited to open for them, he was more excited to see them play for the first time. "We were actually upstairs in an inter-view when they started playing," he says. "They played 'Rock 'n' Roll Star' and then 'Columbia,' and I was just about to jump out of my skin to get down into the room to hear them. And then they started playing 'Fade Away,' and I was like, 'Okay, I've gotta go.' I just ran out of the room, because it was much more important to me to actually see the band than it was to be in whatever the interview was."

Michael laughs. "Yeah, we put a rapid end to the interview at that point, and we all kind of trudged down the stairs after Jason."

"It's rare for a rock band, even then, even in the mid-nineties, to emerge that felt totally believable and credible to me," says Michael. "I knew [Oasis record producer] Owen Morris a little bit. He used to come to my office every once in a while in L.A., and I might be mis-remembering, but he told me a story about going through a bunch of mixes and not being satisfied with the record, playing it back at jet engine–level volume, and finally nailing it. And he told me that one of the guys in the band, maybe Liam, I can't remember, was so excited that he got up and threw a chair through the control room window. The music inspired that level of response in him. That was the energy that came from them and from those records."

Needless to say, the Oasis show made a big impact on Jason and Michael. They were so intrigued by what they had seen and heard that they went to every subsequent show on the Eastern Seaboard on that tour.

# 9:30 CLUB,
# Washington, D.C.,
# October 26, 1994

The Oasis tour continued from Philadelphia to Washington, D.C., where they rolled through the nation's capital to a legendary venue. "The 9:30 Club called and said something like 'This British band, Oasis, is coming to town,'" recalls John Dugan. "Of course, everybody had sort of read about them at that point, and I was like, 'They really want *us* to play with them?'"

John was already playing with a band called Chisel (yes, the beloved nineties indie band), but while they were getting established back in D.C., he was playing in another band called Rollercoaster. "No one's ever heard of it," says John. "We didn't really do much recording." For some reason, they got popular pretty quickly. "We just instantly started getting asked to play all these great shows, which was wild, because usually when you start a new band, it takes forever," he explains. "We played with Low on their first tour, and Oasis, which was amazing." Still, when the 9:30 Club called and offered the opening slot with Oasis, he was a little confused because his band was so new. "I guess we sort of had that loud Gibson-through-Marshall-amps kind of sound, so maybe there was some connection there," he muses. "But I had gone to school in London and I was very up on the British indie scene and sort of following whoever they were hyping that month. So I kind of watched the rise of Oasis, but I hadn't really listened to them a whole lot. They hadn't necessarily hit the States yet, but people were sort of curious about them."

John said yes, of course, and on the night of the show headed to the 9:30 Club, a famously gritty, and even more famously smelly, nightclub that has hosted everyone from the Bad Brains to the Beastie Boys, Justin Timberlake, Bob Dylan, the Foo Fighters, Smashing Pumpkins, and Radiohead.

"I put some friends on the guest list and was just like, 'Let's see what this is all about,'" he says. "We're in this tiny, little greenroom in the basement of the 9:30 Club, and Oasis is right there. So my friends and I were just talking to them. And the thing I've told people whenever they are asking about the brothers or their personalities is that Liam was so gregarious and wanted to meet people and was so friendly and wanted to start conversations. My friend from college was there and she had a button for the Jam and he was instantly like, 'Oh, you guys like Paul Weller!' And he was really gregarious. It wasn't crazy rock and roll times. It was just kind of like an indie show that you play with a big indie band. Even though they were huge in the U.K. at the time, they weren't standoffish or whatever."

While the people seemed nice enough, when it came to the music, John hadn't quite made up his mind. "I wasn't really sure if I was a fan or not, you know?" he says. "I was kind of like reacting a lot to the British press, who had been calling them the Sex Beatles, which I thought was hilariously stupid, but actually made a lot of sense, because they were playing these Beatlesque classic song structures with a little bit of a snarl. But when I heard them, I was like, 'Oh, this reminds me of, like, T. Rex, *Electric Warrior*. There's a little bit of glam rock in there, too, so I was sort of curious about it. They weren't trying to be clever. They weren't trying to be sensitive. Seeing them that first time was really, really crazy in that they were so close and they were so loud. I think Noel and Bonehead had Marshall full stacks, which is the two sets of four speakers, which is so loud. That is plenty loud for an auditorium, but for the 9:30 Club, it was just insanely loud. I just remember it being like, 'Oh my god, this volume is extreme.' After the show, I was chatting with Noel, and I was like, 'Oh my god, you guys were so, so loud.' I'm a drummer, so I mentioned, 'It was great, but you're so loud that I could barely hear the drummer,' and he was kind of like, 'That's okay.'"

After opening for Oasis at JC Dobbs, Michael Howe had driven down from Philadelphia to check out the show in D.C. and he had a similar reaction: "The 9:30 Club, particularly the sound check in an empty room, was absolutely deafening," he says. "It was the loudest thing. It was like standing next to a jet engine or something. I mean, it was just beyond, and I had seen My Bloody Valentine! I had seen a lot of loud shows, and this was on a different level entirely. When the room was filled up, it wasn't so bad, but goddamn, did they play loud."

While John taped most of his shows, he didn't bother taping Oasis. "Which goes to show you, at the time, I was kind of like, 'The jury's out on this band,'" he says, laughing.

Even though he wasn't totally sold on Oasis at the show, a few months later, he was a convert. "I got the promo tape for *(What's the*

*Story) Morning Glory?* around the same time that Chisel was driving around a lot playing shows and doing stuff," he says. "We put that tape on and I think we all were kind of like—I don't want to speak for the other guys—but I was like, 'Whoa, this is really good.' That was the point where I realized it was just obvious that there was greatness there."

# MAXWELL'S,
## Hoboken, New Jersey,
## October 28, 1994

Living in Philadelphia, it was easy for Jason Snell and Michael Howe to pop up and down the East Coast of the U.S. to see bands. So after they opened for Oasis in Philly, they zipped down to D.C. to watch them at the 9:30 Club and then up to Maxwell's, the legendary rock club in Hoboken, New Jersey, and then to NYC's Wetlands, where Oasis was performing for the second time. "We did it for the Charlatans and Adorable, we saw them play at a couple different places, and the Trash Can Sinatras we would go see whenever they were anywhere nearby," says Jason. Michael adds, "I don't know how many other bands that I've seen as many times in as small a window as I did Oasis. I became an A&R guy and worked at record labels for a long, long time, and was out every night, and sometimes saw bands on subsequent nights, but as a fan, I certainly had never done it before, and I don't think I did it after that."

The Maxwell's gig stood out a bit, though, because there was something brewing. "I don't recall what the circumstances were, but there was some controversy, and Evan Dando was there. A bunch of other kind of, you know, alternative musicians. I remember Dando most because I was talking to him a bit in kind of the ancillary room at Maxwell's. And then I think he got on the bus with the band when they left, from what I recall," says Michael. "I don't know what the situation with Liam was, beyond knowing that there was some kind of controversy there."

Arty Shepherd has an idea about the controversy. Arty was a long-time fan of Oasis, having picked up their records (and *NME* and *Melody Maker*) when he was working at Rebel Rebel, an independent record store in New York's West Village. He was pretty instantly a fan and a collector. "I got 'Cigarettes & Alcohol,' like, right when it came out. Epic would come by with promotional stuff, which I collected. Then every cover they were on, in every magazine, I would get. I was also touring Japan at that time and Europe and I would just grab stuff that they were on the cover of. It was crazy. There was a book of their first tour in Japan where they had pictures and I realized that we stayed in the same hotels and played the same clubs, so I re-created a bunch of the pictures." Sadly, he doesn't have any of the photos. "I must have taken nine disposable-camera rolls and I never developed them, like an idiot," he jokes.

So Arty, who later went on to open the cult-favorite metal club Saint Vitus in Brooklyn, was ready to see them play live, even if it meant driving to New Jersey. "The only thing that sucked about Maxwell's, it was impossible to park," he says, laughing. "Fucking Hoboken, man."

It was worth it to see Oasis, though. "The Maxwell's show was pretty crazy," he recalls. "I remember their brother was there, Paul Gallagher, because they shouted him out from the stage, and he was sitting back by the bar. And there was just a *bunch* of people. It was the first time I had witnessed like this weird laddish culture that I didn't really understand at the time. I think most of the Americans that were there didn't understand it, either. There was a lot of English people at the show, and they started doing all these soccer chants. I don't know if it was a City chant or a United chant, but Liam would start arguing with the people who were doing it. It was this whole constant fight, like you constantly felt there was going to be a fight. It was crazy. The energy was outrageous. But they were great, and then when I was leaving, Noel was at the top of the stairs. I played Maxwell's many times and the backstage is down the stairs, so he was at the top of the stairs just saying goodbye to people, saying what's up to people, as they were walking out of the club, which was pretty cool, in retrospect. Oh! And Liam got thrown out of the club. I just know that he was causing some sort of disturbance, and the bouncers threw him out. They were like, 'We don't give a fuck who you are!' So he was on the sidewalk when I walked out and screaming and yelling about something. I was with my girlfriend at the time, and we were just like, 'Okay, what the fuck is going on? This is weird.' I later on met people who worked that night, and they were like, 'Oh yeah, he got thrown out because he was being a fucking asshole.' And I was like, 'Oh, all right, you know, that's Liam.'"

Memory is a funny thing, and when you combine it with time, things can get fuzzy. While both Michael and Arty remember a to-do, the club manager has no recollection of that at all. "We didn't even have a bouncer," says Todd Abramson, Maxwell's longtime booker, club owner, and manager. "Even if it happened and I missed it, I don't see how nobody involved with the band brought it up to me."

That's not to say the night went completely smoothly. A couple of things *did* happen, according to Abramson. "My memories of it are pretty good," he says. "It's one of those nights I went through the ringer."

First, the band was late. "That's not unusual," says Abramson. "I was talking to [their tour manager, Maggie Mouzakitis] during the week, and at that point in time, we had pretty crappy monitors, and when we had a bigger band, especially a British band, as they tended to be a lot more finicky, we would get monitors from SST studio, in Weehawken, that improve things. So I brought up the monitors on the phone with her, and she said they would be fine. And if I knew then what I know now, I probably would have just ignored her and gotten them anyway, but I didn't. And so they roll in, like I said, a little late, and head to the back to set up, and within about a minute, she comes back to the front and goes, 'What are we going to do about these monitors?' Just like, 'Oh, you mean the things that I kept asking you about, and you said they were fine? Those monitors?' Well, thankfully, with SST up the block, we still pulled it off and got the monitors. So first crisis averted.

"Another thing we had that was crappy was the dressing room," he continues. "It was very small and in the basement. There was no bathroom down there. You know, Jon Spencer told me the last time he ever played there, 'If you guys had a bathroom down here, this would be the perfect club,' and I said, 'No, it wouldn't be, because then you'd have to find something else to complain about.' The band was also traveling with a bunch of people, I'll call it a posse. I don't know what they would have called it in the U.K.. I send them downstairs, and then one of those people, I remember him being a somewhat older gentleman, came back up and was like, 'These dressing rooms are rubbish.' Technically, he wasn't wrong."

The band settled in to sound check and then had a little time to kill, and Noel, apparently, went outside. Unfortunately he took his beer with him. "One of the bartenders working that night was Mark Singleton, not a big guy, but very Hoboken. Has a New Jersey toughness about him. Good guy, very straightforward, but didn't really suffer fools," Abramson says. "I guess at one point he looked outside—we had these big glass windows in the front room—and he saw one of the brothers drinking outside, which is a big no-no, probably pretty much everywhere except New Orleans. So he went outside and asked him, 'Are you the singer or the guitar player?' And he responded, 'I'm the guitar player.' So it was Noel. And then Mark proceeded to say, 'Can you play guitar with a broken hand? If not, bring the beer inside.' Clearly a threat. That was pretty funny."

But wait, there's more. "I can't remember the name of the opening band. I do remember they were from Providence. Usually, at worst, an opening band would get a tepid response, you know? More of a lack of response or people just hanging in the front room. This was one of the only nights where the opening act faced hostility. I felt really bad for them, because these people only wanted to see Oasis. And a lot of them were rude. They were English. I'm not saying there's a correlation there. You can decide that. But opening on a sold-out show, some big band that's obviously got a buzz, that's usually a good opportunity, but that night was tough. I remember apologizing to them because I felt bad," he says.

And one more thing: "I don't want to tell you how long I've been doing this. It's about forty years. I think that night was the only time—

I'm not saying I've never worried about a band and what they were going to do—but I just had this sense that these guys are going to steal shit," he says, laughing. "So I stood by the back door where they were going to exit from when it's about time for them to leave. And sure enough, it was pretty hysterical, because I think every member tried walking out of there with something. It was really funny, because it went in sequential order of things getting bigger. I can't remember what two things were in the middle, but the first person tried walking out of there with the pint glass, which I just took out of his hand and put it back. I can't remember the exact order, but it started with a pint glass and it ended with one of them walking out holding a chair in front of him. He maybe tried clumsily putting it under his coat or something, but, you know, I just grabbed it. I mean, I was laughing, but if I had to do it all over again, maybe I would let 'em take it so they can say, 'Oh yeah, I got this at Maxwell's.' "

# WETLANDS PRESERVE,
## New York City,
## October 29, 1994

The final show during the band's first U.S. tour was right where it all started—Wetlands, the small, awkwardly shaped club in lower Manhattan.

Saint Vitus founder Arty Shepherd was there and was struck by how Oasis managed to do so little, but give so much onstage. "They didn't move an inch, which, to me, translates really shitty at Madison Square Garden, but at Wetlands, it was fucking awesome. The songs were incredible. The energy was just coming from the crowd. It was so tense and revved up. It was fucking awesome. They kept the set list really heavy. They played 'Live Forever,' but it was just fucking high-octane," he recalls. "My girlfriend at the time was very pretty, and she finagled her way to the second row. And she sweet-eyed her way to the front to the roadie and he gave her the set list. I got it in the divorce. I've had it with me forever. Every job I've ever had, every business I've ever owned, it's always somewhere in the building, because it's one of those special things that I have always loved.

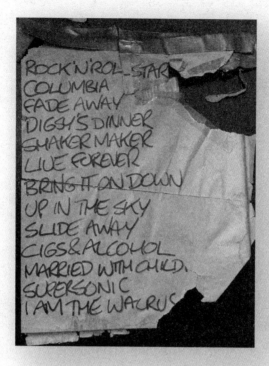

"The coolest part about that show—besides the fucking energy being just incredible—was that they played 'Rock 'n' Roll Star' twice," Arty says. "It was the opening song on the set. And that set list I sent the picture of, it doesn't have it on there. It has it as the first song. So they played 'I Am the Walrus' last, and at the time, they didn't really do encores. For a very long time, they didn't do encores, but the crowd wouldn't leave. And so they came back out, and they were all like yelling at each other or something, like Liam and Noel were screaming at each other about something or other, I couldn't understand them. And then Liam just turns to the microphone and he goes, 'This is what this night's all about.' And they just busted into 'Rock 'n' Roll Star' again, and that was the last song," he recalls. "The show was just fucking incredible. I'll never forget it."

# HAMMERSMITH PALAIS,
## London,
## December 13, 1994

As 1994 wound down, Oasis had returned to the U.K. and had one more concert before the Christmas holiday. They were bringing the *Definitely Maybe* tour to London's Hammersmith Palais. The band was riding high, not only because the holidays were upon them, which meant a very brief break from the road, but because their Christmas single, "Whatever," was near the top of the charts, helping bridge the gap between their debut album and their still-forthcoming second release.

Rob Mason had snagged a ticket to the show early. He had first heard Oasis on the London radio station GLR. "It must have been quite early on because I had all the singles before *Definitely Maybe* was released," he recalls. The string of great music and the high-quality B-sides made him quickly realize they were going to be huge. Back before there was easy access to the internet, fans would sign up on mailing lists to find out about upcoming shows and new releases from their favorite acts. "Whenever you bought a CD or you went to a concert, you normally got a flyer encouraging you to sign up to a mailing list," Rob explains. "Often it was a sort of prepaid postcard you could send back, didn't cost you to join. And so you put in your address, you ended up on a mailing list, and then every so often, you'd get a little postcard from whichever band you'd signed up with to tell you something really was happening, or concerts were happening. So I signed up to that for Oasis and got a few postcards along the way." While Rob can't remember exactly if that's how he knew about the Hammersmith show—or if he found out about it in *Time Out* magazine—he does have a postcard from the Oasis mailing list featuring the concert dates. All he knows is that when he saw there was a show coming up, he got tickets very quickly.

Rob and his friend Lisa headed to the venue on the Tube. "It's been torn down now, but there was a song by the Clash called '(White Man) in Hammersmith Palais,' where it was sort of immortalized," says Rob. "It was a sort-of-punk, sort-of-new-wave sort of venue. It was quite a legendary venue to go to, and all I can remember now is that it seemed really dark inside. I just remember I was quite near the stage for the show, and there's just darkness and the band up there with their attitude onstage. It felt very much like it was you and them, connected. I wasn't really aware of the crowd so much because it was all so dark. That's my recollection, anyway, I might be completely wrong." It has been thirty years, so lapses in memory will be forgiven.

One thing Rob does remember clearly, though, is the encores. "They had a single out called 'Whatever,' which had strings on it, and they had a string section come onstage to perform that song, which I think was the first encore. And then the second encore was 'I Am the Walrus,' you know, the Beatles song, which also has strings. So I really remember the strings on the stage with them and they were very sort of triumphant. They really knew they cracked it that year. It being Christmas and sort of the end of the year, they just seemed really top of the game. And I remember the confidence of the band. I don't remember too much of the rest of the show," he says. "I do remember how Liam Gallagher just stood there motionless, and sort of looked out at the audience. He was kind of the first person to really have that sort of attitude onstage. And I remember that struck me as different and unusual. I think Noel did a solo song or two in the middle of it, as he normally does."

One other thing Rob remembers is this: "It was a really good show. It was a moment. It felt like a moment. And it did feel like it wasn't going to be like that anymore. It was going to be bigger after." He was certainly right about that.

# PART II

# 1995 – 1998

# DEEP ELLUM LIVE,
## Dallas, Texas,
## February 11, 1995

Josh Venable had being doing a radio show in Dallas that was called *The Adventure Club*. "It was on a station there called the Edge that was one of the first alternative stations in America," he explains. "We're in the middle of the country, and we weren't one of the initial stops for a whole lot of British bands coming over. That changed over the years, because of the station." Josh had started working at the Edge while in high school. "In between seventeen and nineteen, I had started being the assistant to the guy that was doing the Sunday night show, *The Adventure Club*, and he quit one day and they let me and another guy, my cohost, take over that show. And then it kind of went from there and I did that show for the better part of almost twenty years in Dallas," Josh says. "According to Noel, it was the first place in America that Oasis was played on the radio. I think there's probably a few different radio hosts that will tell you that it was them. I'm too old to fight with people, so I'll just say, 'Whatever,' but it was early on and I still am extremely proud to have helped bring them to the heartland."

His love for the band wasn't immediate, though. While he had spent a lot of time at Bill's Records in Dallas, flipping through *NME* and *Melody Maker*, and picking up imports, when he heard the first few singles he wasn't that impressed. "I know that's heresy to so many people," he admits. However, when that first record came out, he changed his tune. "I hate to use dumb terms like 'tour de force,' but I mean, there was no one that could deny how good that record was when it first came out, much less the second record. And the Oasis B-sides? I mean, name five great Blur B-sides. No one can do it. Not one person on the planet can do it. But Oasis? When it was 'Acquiesce,' and it was 'Masterplan,' and it was 'Talk Tonight,' and it was 'D'Yer Wanna Be a Spaceman?' and 'Stay Young'? They just kept getting better and better and better."

So Josh was more than ready to see them perform live, which they finally did when they rolled through Dallas on the second leg of the *Definitely Maybe* tour in early '95 to play Deep Ellum Live. Turns out a lot of other people were ready to see them play, too. "[The venue] fit eleven hundred, I think, and you couldn't have fit another person in there with a shoehorn," says Josh. "And it was February in Texas, so it was freezing outside, but it was blazing inside and, god, it was packed.

"Right before the show, I interviewed them on the bus. I was nineteen years old and I couldn't, for the life of me, tell you what we talked about. That thing that you hear about Oasis a lot of the time is that when they're on, it's fights and swearing and throwing things, and then they can switch it off. They were just five guys sitting on a bus quietly sipping tea while a nineteen-year-old interviewed them. And I was scared out of my mind because it was one of the first interviews I'd ever done, and I'm interviewing a band that would go on to be one of the biggest bands on the planet, very, very quickly. I mean, picture that! Being less than a year out of high school and sitting on a tour bus with the band that just put out *Definitely Maybe*. It's mind-blowing to think about, and it's a great memory that I have."

As mentioned earlier, during some of their early tours, Oasis would have local bands open for them. In Dallas, that was a band called Deep Blue Something, best and perhaps exclusively known for their song "Breakfast at Tiffany's," which was having a moment in the nineties. That wasn't the real story of the night, though. Josh recalls, "My story about that night that I'll always remember, and it's kind of become lore in Dallas over the last thirty years or so. I had brought this woman to the show, and it was a woman named Stephanie, and she was very short, okay, I mean, very short, like Yoda tall, Hobbit tall. And we were at the back bar at Deep Ellum Live. And a little person came up and tapped her on the shoulder and said something. He was hitting on her in some way. 'Would you like to go out sometime?' And she said, 'Well, I'm here with him.' He said, 'Is it because I'm a midget?' She said, 'No, it's, it's because I'm here with him.' And his next response, I will never forget, as long as I live—on my child's life—he said, 'If I get onstage, will you go out with me?' She laughed and said, 'Sure, yeah. Go get onstage. Have at it.'

"We go back to ordering our drinks and listening or whatever. This is probably song number twelve or thirteen in the set of fifteen, and we turn around and look up and he is onstage, a little person in between Noel and Liam. Liam looks like he has just seen a ghost. Noel is laughing hysterically because the little person, if you've ever seen *Spinal Tap*, is doing essentially the jig from the *Spinal Tap* 'Stonehenge' number, and he is jigging around in between Noel and Liam. The whole place is singing along with 'I Am the Walrus' while simultaneously their mouths are on the floor, because somehow a little person has just gotten onstage with this band, and at that point, he walks closer to Noel and licks his finger, puts it on Noel's guitar, and goes like the guitar is so incredibly hot that it has burned his finger. So people are crying with laughter. And I mean tears, literal tears—it's like the end of *Terms of Endearment*—tears are like streaming down people's faces. And I will always remember the look on Noel's face as he's just trying to play the outro slash solo of 'I Am the Walrus,' which, you know, was like a nine-minute version of that they would close with on that tour. And so the last four minutes are Noel just wanking around, and the whole time he's staring at this little person standing next to him. And Liam is at the height of his Liam-ing around the stage. It's a visual that I will never forget as long as I live.

"And so that day is always marked in my noodle as interviewing Oasis, Deep Blue Something opening for Oasis, the little person getting onstage after hitting on my date, and then playing 'I Am the Walrus' with a sixth member of Oasis onstage is something. Get somebody to top that story for your book. Cell phones weren't really a thing then, so there's no video footage; believe me, I wish. I would pay so much to have video of that show."

While Oasis may owe Josh a tip of the hat, he owes them one, too. "They were a band that helped legitimize my show, because we were playing them so early that it showed that I knew what I was doing, maybe, by picking that band out of all the thousands of records that I could have been playing that week in that summer of '94," he says. "I got to help spread the word. I did get to turn all those people on to Oasis, because every person in Deep Ellum Live that night in 1995 in February, had probably heard them on my show, and that was fantastic."

# LIBERTY LUNCH,
## Austin, Texas,
## February 12, 1995

Miguel Banuelos has been a Britpop fan for most of his life. "I have a Happy Mondays shirt that I bought in 1986 or whenever it was, through *Rolling Stone*'s back pages, where you could actually buy that, because no one in San Antonio was going to be selling a Happy Mondays shirt," he says, laughing. He also remembers exactly where he was when he first heard the Stone Roses on cassette. "My friend bought it and we listened to it in the parking lot of the record store," he says. So by the time Oasis came around, he was primed to be a fan. "It was very obvious, like, 'Of course, I love these guys, they're perfect, it is exactly what I'm into.'"

In those days, if you wanted to learn about up-and-coming bands from England while living in the middle of Texas, you had to make the effort. "I had read about them in *Melody Maker*, obviously. I read all of those papers from the Tower Records in Austin on the drag," he explains. "When they announced the first tour, I was like, 'Okay, well, obviously I'm going to go.'" He bought a ticket to see them at Liberty Lunch, a revered, now-long-gone indie venue in

Austin. However, Miguel didn't end up seeing Oasis, because the band never showed up. "It's funny, because it fits so well in the folklore of Oasis, but that's the tour that they ended up canceling," he says. "It was the one where Noel went off to San Francisco and left the band. And rumor has it, I don't know if this is proven—this may just be apocryphal—but I guess somebody had given them speed instead of cocaine and they all got, like, crazy, crazy high, way too much. And that caused the problems, and caused, like, people to not show up, and all sorts of stuff. We didn't know any of the other information at the time, we just knew it had been canceled. That gave me an even bigger desire to see them. I'm like, 'Oh no, they could break up before I even get a chance to see them! Oh my god, what's going to happen?'"

Luckily, they rescheduled the tour and came back a few months later. For Miguel there was one small silver lining to the canceled show. "Waterloo Records is the big, independent record store in Austin, and that's where you bought your tickets for Liberty Lunch at the time," he says. "And because Oasis had canceled, as an apology, Waterloo gave away, like, a CD single. If you brought in your canceled ticket, you got a CD single for the first record. That kick-started my love for their B-sides, because, oh my god, their B-sides are amazing! It just happened because of the cancellation. All of these things were adding to my music nerd background. Like, 'Okay, they're a B-side band. They're so volatile, they could end any minute now, but they're also huge and it's all building up.' I ended up convincing, like, five other people to come with me to see them at Liberty Lunch. Tickets were fifteen dollars, so I saw Oasis with maybe two hundred people for fifteen bucks a person. It's hard to explain to people, but it was one of the loudest concerts I've ever been to. I think a lot of it has to do with Liberty Lunch, because it was just a concrete room with a tin top, but it was also them at the time. It was the brick-wall-of-sound thing that they liked to do. Just turn it all up, just all the levels, all the way up, and, you know, leave it in the hands of God to see how it sounds outside. I went with these people, and they were all kind of squares. It was, like, my girlfriend at the time and some friends of hers from her sorority and their boyfriends or whatever, and I remember thinking, 'I hope those people are happy,' because I took them to, like, a pivotal moment in music that they got to see for fifteen dollars. I don't know if they feel that way, but I hope so."

There was one other thing that Miguel liked about the show—the crowd. "Mexicans love British music and love rock music, so, you know, it's Austin, South Texas, like *all* my friends that cared about British music were at that show from San Antonio, as well as Austin. But it's also a music town, so all the music nerds were there," he says. "It was more diverse, I would say, than a usual Austin rock show."

Miguel has now worked in the music industry for years at labels and as a journalist, and seen many, many concerts, including traveling to Oasis shows around the world (more on that later), but this one really sticks out to him. "The palpable menace from that band at that show on that day was just so huge," he says. "The noise was so big, the attitude was so big, the anger was just fully, fully realized. And I guess not anger, but aggression. And so I was like, 'Wow, they were even more than what I thought they were going to be,' because I thought it was going to be a good rock show, but it came off as much more. Just all aura and ambience and personality. That kind of cemented it, and then from that point on, I was like, 'This is basically my favorite band that I lived through.' There're bands before that, you know, I wasn't really old enough for, and there are bands since that are wonderful and I love, but they aren't for me. They are for younger people now, but Oasis at that time and that place was it for me."

# THE MASQUERADE,
## Atlanta,
## February 18, 1995

The first Oasis song I remember hearing was 'Slide Away,' and it was and it still is one of my favorites," says Todd Rivera. "Back in the cassette days, I remember making a cassette tape with just 'Slide Away' on it, on repeat, on both sides, so that I could just listen to that tune."

Oasis was continuing its *Definitely Maybe* tour of the U.S. when they came to Atlanta for the first time. Todd was living there, and the friend who had introduced him to Oasis in the first place bought him a ticket to see them play at the Masquerade, a venue in downtown Atlanta with a capacity of around 1,400. "I would say it was about a quarter full," Todd recalls about the show.

"I thought it was great that Liam pretty much had his back to the audience most of the entire gig," Todd says, laughing. "I just thought, 'Wow, I just can't believe what attitude, but with the tunes that backed it up.' But then they hung out afterwards outside and I just remember Liam being absolutely sweaty and dripping wet and I thought that was great. I just loved the passion. I remember it being quite cold, too. I was quite shocked that the band would even take the time to even entertain conversations with fans outside. I thought that was pretty cool as well." He thought it was cool enough that he ended up going to hundreds more of their shows.

"I followed the *Be Here Now* tour, and *Morning Glory*, though not as extensively because I was, I guess you could say, more broke back then," Todd says. "I was able to see shows that were stateside at least." After Atlanta, he went to the Virginia Beach show, and then traveled up to see them play at Saint Andrew's Hall in his hometown of Detroit. Then he just kept going. Following a band around the country and eventually the world does come with a cost, both financial and professional. "I'd be gone for three weeks at a time or whatever it would be, depending on the number of dates, and my manager said, 'If you leave to go follow this damn band around, you're going to come home to no job,'" Todd recalls. "And they were right."

Even when his wife was pregnant with their daughter, he wanted to follow the band. "I have a picture of us outside at some amphitheater, 'cause even though she was seven, eight months pregnant, I still begged her to load up the car with me, and I know she was uncomfortable, but we still followed the tour. We saw, like, twelve gigs I think during that tour," he recounts. "I just ran across that picture and I told my daughter, 'This is why you're such an Oasis fan. You were listening early on!'"

All the travel and family upheaval were worth it for him to see the band, though. He traveled to London for the Earls Court show, his first time seeing Oasis abroad. While he was there he went to see a football match in Manchester and came back as a Manchester City supporter. He even started a supporters' club in Atlanta to cheer on the team from afar. "I always like to combine my travels if I can, so in the past ten years or so, when I travel over there for the gigs, like Liam's Knebworth gigs, and I've seen Noel in Ireland and all across the U.K. as well, I always incorporate some football match and go to see City as well," he explains.

Over the course of his many, many shows, he has met the band members more than a few times. "I always know that their sound checks are between three and five and Noel would always come out," he says. "Liam, he was definitely more difficult to get to. But one of my fondest memories was at a 1998 *Be Here Now* show, where we hung out extensively at the Four Seasons here in Atlanta before they headed out to the rest of the tour," he says. "I just remember that because I actually spent time with him, just spent time sitting around chatting, but for some reason I had to pick up his tab at the hotel, which is crazy. He's like, 'Oh, we're leaving, we're leaving.' It was the last day of the tour in the United States and I just remember him complaining that he didn't have any currency on him or something, no U.S. dollars or something, so I'm like, 'Okay, I got you.'"

His interactions with Noel were memorable in different ways. "I took my daughter to go see her first-ever concert [a Noel solo show] and he blogged about her on his tour diary and said, 'Yeah, this girl in the front row, this ten-year-old, knew every Oasis song,'" Todd says. "He handed her a letter and it was really sweet, and he signed her phone. And he signed my arm, 'Live Forever,' and I got that tattooed in between the sound check and the concert. But, yeah, Noel's very chatty and remembers all kinds of stuff."

One thing that Todd will always remember was at the Madison Square Garden show: "We did some pregaming before the show," he says. "My wife and I were second row, and we were right behind the

Todd Rivera getting his arm signed
by Noel Gallagher

Olsen twins, and I remember them just getting absolutely hammered, and having to be, like, removed from the gig because they were kind of getting unruly, at least one of them was."

It should come as no surprise that Todd is going to the reunion shows. "I got the Chicago gig, the Toronto, the Jersey, I got some tickets to the Rose Bowl," he says. "Over in the U.K., it was a little bit more difficult." He is hoping that he can sort out tickets and bring his son. "Now that he's seen Noel live, I'd like to see them experience a proper U.K. gig, especially an Oasis one would be super, super special." His son's name? London. "That's just because my wife wouldn't agree to Manchester," he says.

## THE STONE PONY,
### Asbury Park, New Jersey,
### March 3, 1995

Oasis had been touring more or less nonstop through all of 1994 and into 1995. They had started their North America tour working down the West Coast before hitting the middle of the country. Then came a disjointed jaunt from Atlanta to Vancouver to Asbury Park, New Jersey. So they may have been a little extra exhausted by the time they took the stage at the Stone Pony, the legendarily no-nonsense club made famous by Southside Johnny & the Asbury Jukes and a young rocker named Bruce Springsteen.

Arty Shepherd was in the crowd that day. He had been following Oasis around the Eastern Seaboard, starting with their second show at the Wetlands in New York City and Maxwell's in Hoboken. When he saw that they were playing in Asbury Park, just an hour or two (or three depending on traffic) away, he decided to go. "I went with my buddy Adam Blake, who is the bass player of $H_2O$, has been for like twenty-five years," says Arty. "At the time, he was in a Hare Krishna hardcore band called Shelter. And I was like, dude, we have to go see Oasis."

Adam had only recently moved to New York City to play in the aforementioned Hare Krishna hardcore band ("Yes, that's a thing," he says), and was thrilled to go see a band from back home, especially one that he loved.

"I can remember the first time I heard Oasis," he says. "I had got a single on cassette tape, it was 'Supersonic,' and I literally remember being on the train looking out the window, and looking at this view of the London cityscape, and then hearing it and just being like, 'What the fuck was that? I got to hear that again.' I just played it for, like, an hour straight."

When he moved to New York from London, he traveled with a bass case and one bag that included his collection of Oasis tunes. "I knew Arty from my first tour with the Hare Krishna band 'cause he was in the hardcore scene, too. So, of course, when he calls and is like, 'I'm going to the Stone Pony, should I get you a ticket?' I'm like, 'Fuck yeah. I have to see this. I have to see this band.'"

They drove down to Asbury from New York City. "We got there reasonably early," Adam recalls. "I remember seeing the Oasis tour bus. I saw Guigsy walking around, which was kind of cool. And then we went and were, like, right at the stage."

"We're in the front row. It was fucking awesome," says Arty. "Then somebody threw a pint glass at Noel from the crowd, and it broke all over his guitar. Jesus, which, if I understand correctly, is a Les Paul that was given to him by Johnny Marr that was once owned by Pete Townshend, so it was, like, this whole legacy guitar. But I didn't know that till many years later—and I could be totally wrong about that—but it's a great story, and even if it's bullshit I think Noel would appreciate it. So they stopped the show, right? And the security came down, and the guy is screaming at Liam, and Liam's, like, right at the front of the stage, 'I will fuck you up! Meet me at the back door! Meet me at the fucking back door!' And he's like, 'I'm not gonna meet you at the back door. I'm gonna get beat up. Fuck you.' Like, they're just screaming at each other."

"I remember they stopped the set, and Liam was *pissed*," Adam says. "And I think he invited the whole crowd to fight him out back, very British schoolboy.

"So everybody starts chanting, because it was right around when the 'Whatever' single came out—which was a one-off single, only released in England—so only like the real fans knew it. But, you know, this is at the Stone Pony, so it was mostly only real fans there, and so everybody starts chanting, 'Play "Whatever"! Play "Whatever"! "Whatever"! "Whatever"!' Something like that. And Liam and Noel look at each other. Liam walks up to the mic, and he goes, 'You don't deserve it,' and walks offstage. And I was just like, 'That was the fucking best thing I've ever seen.' It was so fucking cool. I didn't give a fuck that they didn't play anymore. I was just like, 'That is the coolest shit I've ever seen.' Like, 'That was fucking awesome.' So, yeah, it was really, really fucking awesome.

"They were amazing," Adam says. "It's years later and, because of what I do for a living, I've seen thousands of hours of live music, tens of thousands of hours, and that one will always stand out."

# SHEFFIELD ARENA,
## Sheffield, U.K.,
## April 22, 1995

April 1995 was a huge month for Oasis. The band had been touring in support of *Definitely Maybe* for two years and it all culminated with their biggest gig yet, at Sheffield Arena. The band also had their first number one hit thanks to "Some Might Say." The relentless touring and singles and press and television appearances had paid off. In just a short amount of time the band had graduated from playing for thirty people in the upstairs room of a pub to playing for twelve thousand fans at Sheffield Arena. It was the first time that "Don't Look Back in Anger" was played live. It was also drummer Tony McCarroll's last gig, as he was let go soon after, due to growing tensions with the Gallaghers. Sheffield Arena, then, became the last show that featured all five original Oasis members. The fans, of course, didn't know that bit. They just wanted to see the band. Unfortunately, the way the arena was set up for the show made that difficult.

Steve Spithray was there, having taken a coach trip from Manchester to Sheffield, and he was not thrilled with the setup in the general-admission area, where fans can usually stand next to the stage.

Not here, though. "We were downstairs in the standing part and it was the first time we'd been anywhere where there was a barrier at the sound desk, so there were two pens of standing. Yeah, we weren't expecting to be stood so far back." Luckily, Steve wasn't the only one frustrated by the setup. "I don't think Liam must have expected it, either, because when he came onstage, right at the start, he was like, 'What's that barrier there?' And he was like, 'You lot at the back, get down here now.' Somebody must have broken through the barrier, and before we knew it, we were all just running through. I mean, the gig would have been stopped if that had happened today, but back then, that was just the Sheffield show."

Iain Huddy, who was tour-managing Ocean Colour Scene, remembers being awestruck by how quickly Oasis had gone from tiny clubs to Sheffield Arena. "I don't know if they had supported some other bands in big venues before, but this was my first time seeing Oasis play to such a crowd. It was like, 'Yeah, they're not playing the usual tour venues anymore,'" he says. "They probably played four-thousand-capacity venues on the tour, but this was Sheffield Arena. This was like ten or twelve thousand, and it was like, 'Okay, this will be interesting to see what it is like to go, you know, from a room above a pub to this. Let's see how it goes down here.' And it just, it just went off. It took the roof off the place. It was absolutely brilliant. Everyone was really buzzing off that. They basically had their mates around them, and we had that feeling that we can do anything. It was just such an exciting gig. It felt like, 'This is really something.'" Oasis had become real rock and roll stars.

# ROLLING STONE CLUB,
## Milan, Italy,
## July 3, 1995

The relentless touring schedule Oasis had undertaken had them playing across Europe, coast-to-coast in the U.S., and sweeping through Japan. It wasn't until mid-1995 that they ever played in Italy, though, and Fabio D'Antonio was ready. However, he didn't have a lot of company in that. "The show had to be moved to a smaller venue due to low presale numbers, as Oasis hadn't exploded in Italy yet," he explains. "I don't have many vivid memories of that night, but one thing I'll never forget is the sound—it was at an incredibly high volume, a wall of noise that was truly immersive. I also remember a brief altercation between Liam and a fan, who tried to hug or touch him, accidentally tearing his shirt. After a quick exchange with the fan onstage, Liam went off to change and returned to finish the show. That early Oasis, the one before they became huge, is the version of the band I feel most connected to and fond of."

In fact, Fabio is very fond of the band. He went on to publish a fanzine called *Wonderwall,* and founded one of the biggest Oasis fan clubs around, known as Oasis FC.

Like many other fans, Fabio first learned of Oasis in the pages of
*New Musical Express*, *Melody Maker*, and other British music magazines. "Oasis were already making a name for themselves on the scene,
with live reviews and growing anticipation around them," he notes.
"At the time, I was also editing and publishing [an Italian-language]
fanzine about Britpop called *Speedway*, so I was deeply immersed
in the British music scene. Since I was already into bands like the
Smiths, the Charlatans, and the Stone Roses, I kept a close eye on the
Manchester music scene. When 'Supersonic' was released, I bought
the single immediately and played it nonstop. I couldn't have imag-
ined then how big they would become or that they'd reach such main-
stream success so quickly. But even before their debut, I already had a
sense that this was a band to watch."

Since he already had a Britpop zine, it just made sense to start
one on Oasis, too. "After Oasis's media explosion, I began receiving
numerous requests for news and lyrics from their first album, which
weren't officially published at the time. It was a completely different
era—the internet was a luxury for few, and information was scarce.
That's when I had the idea to create a dedicated fanzine exclusively
for Oasis," he says. "The fan club officially started in April 1996
with the publication of the first issue of *Wonderwall*. In the first
issue, I compiled lyrics from their first two albums, reviewed their
first Italian live show in 1995, and shared other exclusive content.
Since there were almost no details about the band in Italian magazines and very little communication about their releases, my initia-
tive resonated with fans and received an incredible response. This
success encouraged me to continue publishing periodic issues of the
fanzine."

Fabio didn't stop at a fanzine, though. While the internet was still in its awkward phase, he was working as a web consultant and was able to apply those skills to boosting the Oasis fandom through an online fan club. "This allowed me to spread the word about its existence and gave fans a platform to interact with each other," he says. "I started the fan club because there was a real need for a space where fans could find accurate and accessible information about Oasis. At the time, the only information coming out of the U.K. press was dominated by gossip and stories about the Gallaghers' personal lives, often sensationalized by tabloids camped outside their homes. It frustrated me that their music, and the cultural impact they were having in England, was being overshadowed by negative publicity. For me, the music has always been the most important part of their story, and I've always preferred to discuss the Gallagher brothers in terms of their artistry, not their personal lives."

Fabio's new zine and online fan club were a way for fans to fill the void for information and celebration of the band that brought them all together. "The overwhelming response from fans showed me that there was a passionate community eager to focus on what really mattered: the music," says Fabio.

Eventually the band noticed Fabio's efforts on behalf of the fandom and the online community he was helping create for the band. "[I met them] backstage at their concert at the Forum Arena in Milan in November 1997. I had been invited to show Noel and the band my fanzine, and that's when I first shook hands with and met the members of the group after the show," he recalls. "I remember that Noel entered the backstage after the concert, where we were waiting for him, and he came up to greet me. I was the only male, except for the crew and the band admitted, so it was easy to find me. He thanked me for what I was doing, and that moment felt like a definitive acknowledgment of my work. It was incredibly reassuring to receive Noel's appreciation, especially because what I was doing was all about the music, not the gossip. That moment remains special for me, as it felt like validation for my passion and dedication to promoting the band's music." Fast-forward thirty years and the website is still dedicated to music, occasionally putting out zines and still connecting fans.

# IRVINE BEACH PARK,
## Irvine, Scotland,
## July 14–15, 1995

If you're wondering how the tiny coastal town of Irvine Beach scored an Oasis concert, well, it all starts with a man named Willie Freckleton, who managed a music hall in town.

According to Craig McAllister, a writer and teacher who grew up there, the one thing that helped put Irvine on the map musically was Magnum Leisure Center, which had an old and enormous hall inside it. "Willie Freckleton went to the promoters of tours and said, 'You can have my hall for nothing,' which was unheard of, because it costs you lots of money to hire halls, obviously," says Craig. "So growing up in Irvine, we were blessed every week by seeing a chart band. We had the Jam and the Clash, the Smiths, Madness, Chuck Berry, Thin Lizzy, the Human League, all manner of people just came through the town seemingly every week, and that was due to Willie and the fact that the Magnum had the big hall. Then later, Willie encouraged Radio One, which is a big BBC radio channel, to come and do road shows from the beach park, and it grew and grew and grew to the point where it got Oasis."

By mid-1995, Oasis had been growing and growing on the strength of a string of critically acclaimed and fan-loved singles, a slew of television appearances, and endless touring to support *Definitely Maybe*. However, their sophomore album, *(What's the Story) Morning Glory?*—the one that would make them global superstars—wouldn't be released until October of that year. The only taste fans had of the new material was "Some Might Say," which had been released in April and became the band's first number one hit on the charts.

Craig was working at a record shop in the summer of 1995, and he knew Willie, so he was aware that Oasis was coming to town long before the gig was officially announced. That didn't help him get tickets, though. "The day it was announced, I was in York, in England, doing something with my job, and I missed the tickets going to sale," he says. "All my friends had tickets and I didn't. The happy outcome was that Willie got me tickets. I paid for them, but I managed to get tickets."

When Oasis rolled into Irvine, about forty minutes from Glasgow, they had a number one hit and had just smashed it at Glastonbury. The buzz surrounding them was enormous and fans packed into the tent on the beach in Irvine. "I remember the tent was a seven-thousand-capacity tent. It was absolutely ram-packed. It was sweaty. It was so hot, the sweat was dripping off the ceiling, and it was like rain inside the tent," Craig recalls. The set started with "Acquiesce" and ended with "I Am the Walrus," but for Craig the interesting bit was in the middle. "They did all sorts of stuff from the next album," he remembers. "We were certainly one of the very first places where those new songs were played."

Another memorable moment came when Craig happened to catch Liam's eye. "You know, he does that sort of thousand-yard stare from the stage. I happened to catch his eye and then he stared at me until I had to look away because I was too scared," he says, chuckling.

After the gig, Craig and his friends all went to a local nightclub to relive and recover from the long, hot night. "The Attic was a great place to grow up. They tolerated underage drinkers, and it was a very good place to sort of learn how to drink and be a teenager and maybe put bands on and stuff," he says. "But I remember, after the Saturday night show—they played the Friday and Saturday—but on the Saturday night, me and my friends went to the Attic and I remember there were guys in front of us in the queue singing lines from 'Hello' from the first track of the second album, which they had just heard for the first time at the gig and had really stuck in their heads. Oasis just put our town on the map. It was already a music town, and they sort of drilled in that this is a great place for gigs. And everyone was so hysterically happy that these things had happened."

Craig shared one last memory from the night: "I remember, on the Saturday night, Noel says from the stage, 'Why don't we do this every year? Why don't you write your local MP and sort that out?' And that got a big cheer. Of course, he's never been back."

# BOURNEMOUTH
# INTERNATIONAL CENTER,
## Bournemouth, U.K.,
## October 5, 1995

The gig was scheduled for September 18, 1995, but Blur, who obviously were huge rivals of Oasis, decided to book a gig in Bournemouth on the same night at a different venue," recalls Jo Waghorn. "Instead of going along with it, Oasis were like, 'Nah, actually, fuck this,' and they completely rescheduled the date of the concert. So they moved it to October instead." The shift in dates meant that the gig now came after the release of *(What's the Story) Morning Glory?* on October 2. The album was a smash hit, becoming, at the time, one of the fastest-selling albums in U.K. history. The gig at Bournemouth International Center came right as the band was on the brink of exploding into international superstardom. So it was good that Jo didn't have plans for the rescheduled night in October. "I'm sure we would have canceled any plans we had anyway, because it was quite a big thing really. They were probably on my list of favorite bands by that point," he says. "We were just really excited."

Jo and his friend Gareth were massive Oasis fans. "I had the first album on cassette tape, and I just loved it," he says. "And we were like, 'We should definitely go and see them when they next tour.' Before the second album came out, we managed to get tickets for their *(What's the Story) Morning Glory?* tour."

They found out about the show in the pages of *NME* or *Melody Maker*, where they would list the tour dates of the band. "Then you would phone up the venue or some sort of ticket hotline, and you would get your parents to pay for them on their credit card, and then they would send you the tickets in the post, and then you would take your tickets to the show," he explains. The ticket to Bournemouth was £10.

A friend's mom drove them to Bournemouth from where they lived in Farnborough and they had an amazing night, pushing their way near the front. "I was fifteen at the time, and going to gigs when you've just started going to gigs is always so much more exciting," he says. "I remember someone threw a shoe onstage and Liam got a bit lairy about it and threw it back, if I remember correctly."

It was also fun hearing songs from the new album played live. "The album had only come out two or three days before we went to see them play, so it was like a lot of material they were playing was stuff that no one had ever heard before," he says. "I remember hearing the song 'Round Are Way,' which was one of the B-sides, and just being like, 'This is crazy, I've never heard this song before, and now it's ingrained in my head.'"

After the show, they were able to say they were early fans. "It was kind of nice watching them become bigger and bigger," he says. "Also, that tour we saw them on was the last time they ever played small venues. It was a few thousand people, but after *Morning Glory* came out and they became astronomical, the only places you could see them play were, like, stadiums or arenas. It was just really cool to be in a venue where you didn't have to look up at a screen to see who was playing. You could stand not that far from the stage and see, like, Liam Gallagher and Noel Gallagher in person. It was just amazing."

While Jo did see them play a few more times, it was that early gig that he looks back on most fondly. "The best thing about seeing Oasis in '94, '95, was the audience," he says. "The audience back then was like ninety to ninety-nine percent full of teenagers, young people, and it was just a really nice buzz, really nice atmosphere. Ten or fifteen years down the line, when they're playing the places they played in the 2000s, I've heard from people that it was just not a very nice place to be. Really toxic, full of, like, thuggish blokes and had a football-hooligany-type atmosphere. Whereas when we saw them— and I went to Knebworth as well—it was just loads of kids having a really good time. And it was just a really beautiful experience."

Despite his love of the band in its early days, he has no interest in going to the reunion shows.

"Firstly, I don't want to spend three hundred quid on the ticket," he says. "Secondly, I don't want to see anyone play at Wembley Stadium *ever*. I could watch it on YouTube. Unless you're at the front, you may as well be in a different room. It's gigantic. Thirdly, I don't really like people, but I really don't like Oasis fans." He pauses a moment. "That's quite a sweeping generalization, really, considering the amount of people that are going, and I'm not really a horrible person!"

For him, he saw them at what he considers their prime and doesn't want to look back. "It's not really Oasis, is it? It's Liam and Noel and whoever else they're gonna get to play with them," he says. "For me, Oasis were of a certain time, and that time was the mid- to late nineties."

# EARLS COURT,
## London,
## November 4–5, 1995

The first time Victoria Watson saw Oasis was on December 30, 1994, at Middlesbrough Town Hall during their *Definitely Maybe* tour. It was the band's last show in the U.K. before leaving for their first U.S. tour. She was fifteen and loved everything about Britpop. "It really spoke to me and my friends at school. We wanted to go to gigs and wear the kind of clothes the singers and their fans wore," she recalls.

"One of my best memories was at the Earls Court show in 1995, when I called my boyfriend from a pay phone in the venue when 'Wonderwall' was playing, which was one of our favorite songs," she says. "I was sixteen at the time of the concert and had come down to London from Durham with my best friend. Her parents drove us to London specifically to see the concert! It was the biggest venue I had been to at that age, so it was a magical experience, and, yes loud, though we were at the back of the venue. The energy was amazing."

As the band worked their way through the recently released *(What's the Story) Morning Glory?* Victoria knew what she had to do. Despite the fact that there were around twenty thousand fans crammed into the space while a famously loud rock band played, she needed to call her boyfriend. Since this was before most people had cell phones and streaming and video recording were a decade away, the only option was to call him on the pay phone. "The pay phone was inside the venue to the side of the stage. I remember when they started playing 'Wonderwall,' it felt like such a monumental moment I just had to go and ring my boyfriend so he could hear the song live, as he was also a fan." No word on whether her boyfriend appreciated the gesture or even heard a lick of it.

# KOME ALMOST
# ACOUSTIC CHRISTMAS,
## San Jose, California,
## December 16, 1995

Nicholas Hunt, now a true crime writer, was interning at San Jose's alternative radio station KOME just as Oasis started to hit it big in the U.S. He was born in the U.K., but raised in San Diego, so he tried to stay up to date with what was happening in the music scene in England and knew about the band. "Oasis was just so damn catchy. The early stuff was so catchy, and I was so into it, and nobody knew who they were," he recalls. That's why he was excited to see them on a lineup for a show that his radio station was sponsoring called Almost Acoustic Christmas, where the band would play, as the name suggests, almost acoustically. The lineup, according to the internet, included Everclear, Garbage, Jawbreaker, No Doubt, Radiohead, Sonic Youth, the Rentals, Toadies, Tripping Daisy, and, in the middle of it all, Oasis.

"And this is late '95, so they were probably already recording *Be Here Now*. They were well established in the U.K.. They were already super famous. They were household names. But in the USA, they weren't really. So everybody was flying out to see

Radiohead," he says. "I was actually there to see a local band from my area called No Doubt. Oasis were kind of a middle act in this lineup."

While Nicholas was there to see No Doubt, just breaking through with "Don't Speak," he was excited for the rest of the lineup, too, particularly Oasis. "There were a lot of big bands playing and Oasis was just one of them, but as soon as they hit the stage, I was like, 'This is the business,'" he says. "Like, this is really the way to do it, because they didn't really give a shit, like the rest of them. I mean, they did, you know. They played their set, and all the songs are catchy. And even if you haven't heard the songs before, you feel like you have, if you know what I mean. And if you were an Oasis fan, like I was, you played that album to death. And this is back in the day when people actually listen to albums, not, you know, two-point-five-minute songs on Spotify. You listened to that album and you listened to it to death, so you knew every single word of every single song. But this was kind of acoustic. When I say kind of—for those who are old enough to remember *MTV Unplugged*—it was generally one person playing acoustic and the drum didn't have loads of mics on it, so it wasn't really acoustic, it just kind of was. I think the thing that was best about that show was that I didn't really realize what I was seeing: this was Oasis playing an acoustic set."

The following year, in August 1996, Oasis performed a similarly almost-acoustic set on *MTV Unplugged* in a London music hall. Liam reportedly had a sore throat and couldn't perform, so Noel stepped in, accompanying himself on an acoustic guitar. The performance Nicholas witnessed had Liam performing as Noel strummed, a rarity.

Although Oasis wasn't the main draw for him that day, he did go see them play several more times, including twice at Wembley, once in Manchester, and at least one more time after that. While the big shows were fun, none beat seeing them sandwiched between Everclear and Tripping Daisy on a college campus in the nineties.

# LAKEWOOD CIVIC AUDITORIUM,
## Lakewood, Ohio,
## March 2, 1996

A s Oasis continued their *(What's the Story) Morning Glory?* tour across the U.S., they found themselves where few ambitious young bands want to be: in a high school auditorium in suburban Cleveland, Ohio. Marah Eakin, though, was really, really glad they were there. "I think everyone has those bands that, like, hit right when they're thirteen to fourteen and becoming a very sentient music listener and a person that's making their own opinions," she says. "For me Oasis just happened to hit that spot."

As a self-professed "Beatles dork," Oasis resonated with her when she heard them on Cleveland's alternative rock station, 107.9 The End. Marah bought the album at Borders, as kids in the nineties in Middle America did. Then she saved up her Easter money and whatever money her grandma gave her to hit the record store in the mall to buy posters and "the skinny little import singles." "I think I had everything that came out," she recalls. She would play them on the CD boom box in her room and decorated her room with Oasis art. "I wasn't allowed to put posters on my wall, because we had wallpaper," she says. "But I could put them on my doors, so I had multiple Oasis posters on my doors." She was obsessed, so when she heard they were coming to town, of course she had to go.

To get tickets for the show, there was only one place to do it: the grocery store. Marah's dad went to the store the day the tickets went on sale and picked up four. "But I couldn't get four people to go," she remembers. "I could only get one other person to go. So, my dad sold the other two to some people from his work and my friend Shelly and I had to sit by my dad's coworkers for the show."

The concert was held at the Lakewood Civic Auditorium, which was in fact a high school. "It's in a western suburb of Cleveland, and is inside a school. It's like a two-thousand-kid high school, but I don't even know what the capacity of that auditorium is, but it couldn't have been huge," she recalls. As an eager young fan who had never been to a concert before, Marah knew she wanted to be there early. "We got dropped off and it was, like, doors open at seven, so we got there at five thirty," she says, laughing. "We waited in line, and then we got in, and I remember being, like, in the second row, maybe third row, very good seats. They were, by the way, ticketed, so it wasn't like we had to get there early to find a seat. Still, I just thought it was all really amazing. This shitty local band opened up called New Salem Witch Hunters, and I remember Oasis were like, 'Wow, weren't they great?' I remember thinking, like, 'Oh wow, they thought they were bad, too.' Just the attitude. It was the same Oasis you saw on TV. A lot of stage presence, but also no stage presence. I just thought they were great. They closed with 'I Am the Walrus,' and I was like, 'Whoa.' Eventually I read that they always close with that, but at the time and being a Beatles dork, I thought it was really amazing. They also had the mid-set thing where the band leaves and Noel does, like, three songs. It was standard Oasis, but I thought it was amazing."

After the show Marah called her dad ("We had to do that thing where you call your parents from the pay phone and let it ring one time or whatever and that's the signal for them to come get you") and then she and Shelly hung out as long as they could, trying to see if they could meet the band. "We were like, 'Oh, I want to talk to them' and whatever, but also you're fifteen and you think you're very cool, but you realize now as a forty-year-old that would be very creepy," she says, cracking up at the thought. "My dad told me later that his coworkers had met the band and got invited to hang out with them, and went to a bar with them and stuff. And I remember being *so* mad. I was like, 'Goddamn it,' just so upset about it. Like, 'That could have been me,' but no, it couldn't have."

While she didn't get to the meet the band, the concert opened up a whole new world to Marah. She started going to more concerts, including more Oasis gigs, and taking a deeper dive into the wide world of music. "It made me start reading *Mojo* and going to Borders to sit in the aisle and read copies of *Q* that are eleven dollars or something, which I still bought," she says. It also helped her realize there was a broader community of music fans she could fit in with. As she got older, she found college radio and eventually music journalism, where she has worked ever since. "In many ways, I like to draw a line directly to Oasis—I mean, I guess I could draw it to the Beatles or to whoever—but Oasis happened to be the first show I saw and the first, like, modern band that I got obsessed with." Despite a decades-long career as a music journalist, though, Marah has never interviewed Oasis.

"There's part of me that's like, 'I'm the best person for this job, because I know so much about this.' But then there's also part of me that's like, 'But I don't want them to think I'm not good at asking questions and then be mean to me, and I'll be crushed,'" she says. "It's too personal."

# SNOASIS,
## Great Gorge Ski Resort,
## Vernon Valley, New Jersey,
## March 9, 1996

aniel Ralston, a writer, documentarian, and podcast producer, remembers exactly when he fell in love with Oasis. "My best friend Mike Black and I were at the Wall, a chain of CD stores that was incredibly easy to steal from, and I was debating between two recent releases, *(What's the Story) Morning Glory?* and *Resident Alien* by Spacehog, a one-hit wonder fronted by a Scott Weiland look-alike who went on to marry Liv Tyler. 'Wonderwall' and 'Hog's 'In the Meantime' were both gigantic songs at the time. I like to imagine somewhere there's a parallel-universe version of me who bought *Resident Alien*. He's probably in prison for wire fraud or heroin possession. I opted for *Morning Glory* and Oasis has been my favorite band ever since, except for the week after SNOasis, the worst show I've ever attended."

Ralston and his friends, high school juniors at the time, had learned that Oasis was playing a ski resort in New Jersey, an hour and a half from their hometown of Allentown, Pennsylvania. Specifically, a Z100-sponsored concert at Great Gorge Ski Resort in Vernon Valley, New Jersey. "I was intimately familiar with Great Gorge Ski

Resort, the site of SNOasis, because, in the summer months, it was known as Action Park, a wildly dangerous amusement park that featured a waterslide with a full loop, and a host of other death traps that the management called 'rides' and staffed with stoned teenagers," Ralston says, recommending the documentaries about the notorious family fun center lovingly referred to as Class Action Park. "As you can imagine, the owners of Great Gorge put very little care into the grounds, and the winter incarnation of the small hill they called a ski resort was a bare-bones operation compared to any other ski resort on the planet."

The show included an extremely mid-nineties rock billing: Garbage, Stabbing Westward, God Lives Underwater, and Oasis. ("A thousand scientists working in a lab for a thousand years could not create a more nineties lineup," Ralston jokes.)

"We tuned in to Z100 on the way to the ski resort hoping to hear 'Wonderwall' or 'Champagne Supernova,'" says Ralston. "The over-caffeinated DJ was hyping SNOasis during every commercial break and his enthusiasm for this 'once-in-a-lifetime alt-rock event' was the place to be for anyone lucky enough to be within driving distance of Great Gorge."

While Black and two other friends who'd tagged along spent a few hours on their snowboards terrorizing skiers, Ralston staked out a spot near the stage for the SNOasis festivities. "Mike and our friends, all pink-faced and coursing with adrenaline from knocking over old people on the slopes, joined me near the stage as the first act, God Lives Underwater, hit the stage," recalls Ralston. "They played for a half hour and their low-key electronica failed to whip the cold crowd into a frenzy. We were all there to see Oasis." Stabbing Westward fared slightly better, according to Ralston. "Their only flaw was never writing a decent song, and they remain one of the era's least interesting bands, sounding like Creed without the hooks or Stone Temple Pilots without the drug-induced danger," he says. Next up was Garbage, who were ascending the charts almost as quickly as Oasis thanks to frontwoman Shirley Manson. "I think it was her Scottish roots and hard-as-fuck demeanor that seemed to make her impervious to the cold," says Ralston. "She stalked the freezing stage in a short black dress and smeared her bloodred lipstick across her face." The way Ralston remembers it, it was when Garbage finished their set they got their first sign that the Oasis show they were about to watch was not going to plan. "Shirley thanked the crowd and said, 'Noel Gallagher is up next.' Thanks to my excessive music magazine consumption I knew Noel was the band's songwriter and de facto leader, but I found it odd that she would introduce Oasis as just 'Noel Gallagher.' The next bad omen was the stage itself. As the sun was setting, the road crew cleared Garbage's huge amp stacks from the stage. Then the stage sat bare for what seemed like an eternity. By this point, Mike and I were commiserating about the fact that at this point, there should have been . . . something going on. Where was Bonehead's amp? Why wasn't Alan White tuning up his drum kit? Our answer came when a lone roadie placed an acoustic guitar stand in the center of the stage along with a folding chair and a microphone. The mic stand was bent at its elbow to accommodate a seated singer, not Liam, who famously likes his mic stand straight and a foot above his head so he can open his throat and project. With the stage set for one, the crowd began to murmur and turn listless as another half hour passed. Finally, Noel Gallagher took the stage in a hooded, goose-down jacket holding his Takamine acoustic guitar. The crowd cheered half-heartedly and he clearly realized that this—an acoustic set from a guy who was in Oasis, but not the impossibly good-looking singer with the magic voice—was not going to be an easy gig. Without a word, he took his seat, blew onto his freezing-cold hands, and did the only logical thing he could to appease the crowd: he played 'Wonderwall.' It was lovely, and Noel's version of the song remains on par with the recorded version sung by his kid brother. Despite the switcheroo, the crowd sang along, and for those four minutes, the show delivered. That would be the last moment of joy before everyone in attendance turned on Noel and, by association, Oasis."

You know the joke about the food being bad and there not being enough of it? Well, that's how the set was, according to Ralston: "Thirty seconds into his next song, 'Cast No Shadow,' Noel abruptly unplugged his guitar and slinked off the stage. He didn't address the crowd. He just left. We waited for his return, but after ten minutes of screams and snowballs flying toward the empty stage, a Z100 employee took the stage with the thankless task of telling us that Noel would not be returning and the show was over." It was too cold for a riot, so the crowd just left, grumbling as they went. It was depressing for Ralston, and as he and his frozen friends piled into the car to leave, he made a decision, ejecting his copy of *Morning Glory* from the car's CD player, rolling down his window, and chucking it into the freezing New Jersey night.

Ralston's frustration with Oasis didn't last too long. He started warming up to them again after reading a blurb in *Rolling Stone* magazine at Borders that the extreme cold had "caused Noel's fingers to freeze to the fretboard of his acoustic guitar." A year later, he and

Mike went to see Noel perform solo again, this time at the Tibetan Freedom Concert on Randall's Island in New York City. "He played five songs, including the debut of his fuzzed-up cover of the Beatles' 'Helter Skelter,'" Ralston recounts. "Mike and I were in the front row and our lifelong Oasis fandom was resurrected."

# CARDIFF INTERNATIONAL ARENA,
## Cardiff, U.K.,
## March 18–19, 1996

James Corcoran is glad he got to see Oasis when he was fifteen and they were playing in Cardiff. "It was the last run of gigs before the huge summer shows in 1996, Knebworth and the related shows. So it was the last run when Noel was still doing an acoustic set. And so that was really great," he says. "It was just an incredible experience. It was the closest to death I've ever been, because you're just the throng. It's different in America, where it's, like, about moshing and kind of bouncing into each, whereas in the U.K., it's just a crush. It's like the football terrorist crush and I thought I was going to die a number of times. You think, 'I have to step out now, I have to step out, it's too much, it's too much,' but then 'Roll with It' kicks in and you're like, 'Oh no, I've got to get back in.' It was just so insane. An incredible gig." It's not just the thrill that he got to have a near-death experience while seeing the band in their prime, it's also that it gives him just a little extra cred when talking to Oasis fans and the community on *The Oasis Podcast*.

James came about his fandom in the classic way—a friend's cooler older brother. "A friend of mine made me a tape. His older brother had really gotten into Oasis and he was the legend that had these recordings and he would make you a tape," he says. "I had a cassette tape with *Definitely Maybe* on one side and the B-sides on the other side. And that was just like, 'Wow, this is the best band I've ever heard,' and it changed my life from there."

James saw a lot of the popular bands in the nineties—Pulp, Cast, Ocean Colour Scene—but Oasis always stood out to him. "There was an extra level of aura," he says. "Everything else was great, but this was just on another level that you just can't even explain." As he grew up and added new songs and bands to his listening rotation, he always had a spot for Oasis. When podcasts started becoming more popular, he kept waiting for someone to make one about them. "I would refresh iTunes every few months, thinking there must be an Oasis one out there," James says. "And certain people started doing a few Oasis-related interviews, but there was no Oasis-dedicated podcast. And so it came to the point where I just thought, 'Well, I'll give it a go.'" James started *The Oasis Podcast* in 2017 and had fairly low expectations for the show. "At first, I thought it might just be my friends, sharing our Oasis memories and top tens and all that sort of stuff. But then I just started emailing people that I thought might be willing to talk to me and would be interesting. Within the first fifteen or so episodes, I'd interviewed an original band member in Tony McCarroll; Brian Cannon, who's done the artwork; Mark Feltham, who played the harmonica on a number of their recordings—like some really big, important names in the history of the band. So having very little experience or research or anything, it just sort of happened from there."

In all the years he has been doing the podcast, there's one interview—one person—that particularly stands out to him: Mary

McGuigan, Guigsy's sister. "She died just before Christmas," he says. "She was incredible. Because Guigsy hasn't really done interviews since the band split up, Mary was almost like the spokesperson for Guigsy. So she was always the one defending him online for all these years. If someone, like, slagged off his bass playing or questioned, 'Did he really play on the albums?' or something, Mary might pop up and say, 'You know he did.' So she was absolutely amazing and a real force for good."

Aside from being siblings with an original band member, Mary is also a key figure in Oasis lore on her own. "She may have been responsible for some of the original Rain song lyrics before Noel joined the band," says James, referencing the original incarnation of Oasis, before Noel joined and the name changed. "There's a song called 'Rooftop Rave,' which is about the Strangeways [prison] riots, and I was sort of talking to her about that, and she's like, 'What's that song about? Me and our kid wrote that song, and we wrote the lyrics together. I remember seeing it on the telly and writing it.' It's like, wow! It's such good fun when you get a little moment like that. That was a really special one, Mary. The latest edition of this [Official Oasis Podcast] book that we're doing, we're going to dedicate to her. She's an incredible person. It's just devastating that she's gone."

At this point, James is over three hundred episodes into the podcast. While it was always a hit, the band reuniting means the podcast is more relevant than ever, as more and more people want to talk about Oasis and listen to other people talk about them, too.

———

When Oasis stopped in Cardiff on their *(What's the Story) Morning Glory?* tour, it was the first chapter in a love story of a young couple who found a band they adored—and a son who learned to love them, too. It all started, as many great stories do, in a pub. This one in Caerphilly, Wales. "My mom said they were at the pub and 'Wonderwall' came on the jukebox and, originally, my father didn't like the band at all. He said, 'This is sort of rubbish.' But my mother, she went out and bought the CD, and then she was obviously playing it in the house. And it sort of grew on my father," says Jake McCarthy. His father, Kevin, eventually became known as the biggest Oasis fan in the world.

"My mom, Lisa, told me that everybody from the pub, they all managed to get some Oasis tickets to go and watch them in a gig in Cardiff," Jake says. When Oasis came back to Cardiff the following year, Kevin and Lisa went to that gig, too.

"Then my mom and dad were walking home, but they seen a lot of people following . . . well . . . something, so they sort of just followed the crowd," says Jake. Turned out the crowd was heading to the hotel where Oasis was staying. "My dad was a bit sneaky, so he snuck into the hotel and bumped into Liam in the lobby. He had a chat with Liam, then he got my mother in. And they were all talking. Then they were at the bar in the hotel with Liam and Bonehead and Guigsy. They were just chatting, and ended up being in the bar all night, basically. And it went from there."

A few months later, Kevin and Lisa borrowed a car from one of Kevin's friends and traveled up to London. "I'm guessing they wanted something to do and decided to look for where Oasis lived, because obviously they had started following them even more after they met them," says Jake. "So they found where Liam lived, and they seen him, and he recognized them from Cardiff. So he asked them, like, 'What are you doing up in London?' And my dad just wanted to get some things signed. So it took off from there."

Jake's dad was a real collector. "Anything that was to do with Oasis in the newspaper, my dad would cut out and keep, and then he would frame them," Jake says. "I've got, like, thousands of newspaper clippings just boxed up. A lot of them are signed as well." His dad was also an avid photographer, snapping photos everywhere he went, including to visit the band members.

Back to that first trip to London, though: "My mom told me that when they bumped into Liam in the morning—he was with Patsy Kensit at the time, and I think they had a bit of a fiery relationship—so Liam said to my father, 'We're going shopping, we'll be back later.' When they got back, the windows were smashed on the car. My dad took pictures. They'd been mobbed by fans, who ended up smashing the back window of the car. So when Liam and Patsy pulled back up to the house, the press were there, and they were asking, 'What's happened? Why is the car smashed?' And they were trying to sort of get my dad to do an interview saying that Patsy had smashed the car window, when it wasn't actually her, it was just, like, some fans had done it. So they were trying to pay my father to basically say she smashed the window. They were just trying to get a headline out of him. They were then trying to buy the pictures from him as well, because he had obviously had the photo before when the car was fine, and then the photo after the car was smashed. Then my parents went to Noel's house the same day. They were just randomly looking for it and they bumped into him outside his house as well. So they got more stuff signed by Noel. I think that was the first time they'd seen them where it was not at the gig, it was at their house."

At some point someone in the band's entourage or management got his father's contact information and a woman would contact his father and send him VIP passes and tickets for the shows. "They were just on the guest list basically throughout the band's entire career," Jake says. His father kept everything—ticket stubs, passes, all of it—which is now part of the collection. "They're in a frame," he says. "Some of them are signed."

During the four-year period around the release of *Morning Glory* and *Be Here Now* and after, Kevin and Lisa would head to London and visit outside one of the Gallaghers' houses. "They would chat to them outside regularly, and they would go to, like, a pub nearby with Noel and would have a few beers with them, which is pretty cool," Jake says. Jake's mom has a theory that the reason Oasis was so welcoming to his parents is because they were older and married, they had kids of their own, and they "weren't crazy when they seen them" and weren't "just being maniacs chasing them around the place." That could explain why when Kevin and Lisa decided to drive to France and pitch a tent outside the remote château where Oasis was recording *Standing on the Shoulder of Giants*, the band didn't freak out when they saw them. Instead, they gave them some beers and came out to chat and sign some more items for Kevin's expanding collection.

Because they were camped outside the château, his parents were there the night Bonehead quit. "My mom said it was the early hours in the morning and they heard the gates opening and a car driving off," says Jake. "It was Bonehead leaving. That was his last time with the band. He was gone."

It was a blow for the band. While it was initially reported that Bonehead had left to spend more time with his family, in *Forever the People: Six Months on the Road with Oasis*, their longtime biographer, Paolo Hewitt, claimed otherwise: "It was guitarist Bonehead who precipitated a crisis by drunkenly breaking into producer [Mark 'Spike'] Stent's room at 4am. The subsequent row saw Bonehead pack his bags and fly back to Manchester."

When *NME* broke the story that summer, Noel Gallagher famously quipped that Bonehead's departure was "hardly McCartney leaving the Beatles." Whatever the reason for the departure, the McCarthys had a front-row seat for it. They snapped a photo as he drove off into the night.

Less than two weeks later, Paul "Guigsy" McGuigan, the bass guitar player, faxed a resignation letter to the band. "No one is bigger than the band," *The Guardian* reported Liam Gallagher saying in a press conference. "Unless one of us was 15 feet tall, then he would be a lot bigger." At the time, the Gallaghers speculated that Guigsy and Bonehead didn't want to be away from their families for months as Oasis once again toured America. The McCarthys, however, were happy to follow the band to the States.

Jake and his brother stayed in Wales with their grandparents, proudly telling folks that their parents were touring with Oasis. "I was cool at school because of it, because everyone liked Oasis then, and I sort of got off saying, 'Oh, my dad knows them,'" Jake says, laughing.

Jake explains that his mother struggles with anxiety, which is why he's doing the interview and not her. That anxiety was partially triggered by his father getting nearly crushed at an Oasis gig, and the resulting anxiety is why Jake and his brother went to only one show—the Y100 Festival in Philadelphia, at the First Union Center. "I was really young, so I can't remember exactly, but there was Moby, Foo Fighters, Beck, some other band, and Oasis," he says. [Ed. note: *The other band was Stroke 9, which he will be forgiven for forgetting.*] The main thing Jake remembers from the show is the most older-brother thing ever: "I remember my brother slept the entire time." The next day, Oasis was playing some acoustic set at a radio station and Jake's dad had reached out to Noel and gotten an invitation. "There was only maybe ten or twenty of us in the room listening to them do this acoustic session, which is pretty cool. And then Noel gave me and my brother the plectrums for his guitar, which I've got them, but I can't find them. At the time, we were collecting Pokémon cards. So they both signed some Pokémon cards for me and my brother, which is quite cool as well. That's sort of my first memory of them."

But Jake's favorite moment with the band came a little later. "My dad took me to Noel's house, and we went for some beers with Noel. I didn't drink beer because I was maybe nine, but it was quite crazy," he says. "At the time, I didn't think anything of it because I was only a kid, but my dad went for a pint with Noel, Kate Moss, Jude Law, and Sean Bean, which if you tell anyone that, they wouldn't believe you. But yeah, that happened."

The last time Jake's parents saw Oasis together was at Glastonbury in 2003. "They managed to get VIP tickets into Glastonbury, and they were staying near where Noel was staying," Jake says.

His parents split up, but his dad continued following Oasis, traveling to Vegas with them as well as a recording studio in Cornwall. "I looked online and it says it's Sawmills Studio, which is where they recorded the first album, but it was well after that point, so I don't know why they were recording down there, but I've got loads of pictures of it," Jake says. [Ed. note: They had likely gone to start work on *Don't Believe the Truth*.] "That's all I know, because I can't ask my father anything else, which is a shame." Kevin McCarthy passed away in 2017. He was only forty-two. Jake doesn't think the band knows what happened to his dad. The family played "Whatever" at his dad's funeral and his tombstone is engraved with the words "Live Forever."

# BILL GRAHAM CIVIC AUDITORIUM,
## San Francisco,
## April 13, 1996

There's a patch of sidewalk in San Jose that Ericha Fabay is particularly fond of. That's because she once slept on it while waiting in line to get tickets to see Oasis at San Francisco's Civic Auditorium.

The show came in the middle of the U.S. tour in support of *(What's the Story) Morning Glory?* The booking agent for the tour had routed the band down the West Coast at the end of 1995, then over to Europe for January, back to the U.S. for February and March, over to Europe again, and then back to the U.S. in April, and then a few months off after the shows at Maine Road. If the band was tired, which they likely were, it didn't show at the concert, or at least not enough for Ericha to notice.

"It was such a phenomenal show," she says. "The vibe, the people, just lots of fun. The Civic [Auditorium], historically, doesn't have the best sound, but it didn't matter because of the way they played and the way everyone came together, the excitement, the joy, the music, they just were so *on*. It was a phenomenal show. Even getting kicked in the head, I didn't feel stunned by that at all. I just felt it was kind of like an anointment." Yes, she was kicked in the head by someone crowd-surfing past her, but she didn't mind, because she was watching her favorite band. Plus, she had already slept on an inflatable mattress on a sidewalk to get the tickets, so what was a little kick in the head?

At the end of the show, Ericha waited around the venue until the wee morning hours in hopes of trying to meet the band—and she pulled it off, finding them outside the show. "They were funny. They were really joyful, too, and also taken aback by everything that was going on. I remember having a portable little camera and me getting a picture with Bonehead and getting to see Noel and Liam and Guigsy and [new drummer] Alan White. And, you know, Liam being chased around by girls. It just was fun to see."

She had discovered the band thanks to MTV's *120 Minutes*, San Francisco's Live 105 radio, and a group of friends with great taste. "I would scrape together a lot of money to buy the British magazines such as *Q* and *Select* and *NME* to read about them and what this band was about," Ericha recalls. "I respected that they were going to do it their way. It was definitely a DIY, like, 'Don't even make an attempt to try to mold us.' It felt good, it felt acknowledging, and it felt like something I could relate to as a younger person. And it just made things so fun."

Since that first gig in San Francisco, Ericha has seen Oasis play twenty or twenty-five times, she can't quite remember. "I'm very grateful that I got to see them. Extremely grateful," she says. She is also grateful that she has met the band on many, many occasions and gotten them to sign a few memorable things for her. "One issue of *Select* magazine came with a little Liam blowup doll—I mean, I know that sounds not very nice—but it was a little doll and so I had Liam sign it, and he was laughing," she recalls. While some of her collection was stolen out of a storage locker, she still has a few cherished items. "I have all of the original record releases by Oasis, and all of the singles and various country's releases that are particularly difficult to get of certain songs, like I have a promo from, I believe it's France, of 'Slide Away.' It's beautiful," she says.

Over the years she has honed the art of meeting the band after the show, estimating that she's met them thirty times or so over the years. "The brothers have always been very nice to me and my crew. I appreciate that as well as, you know, Gem [Archer], Bonehead, Guigsy, Allen, even Zak [Starkey] and the other members of their individual touring bands. They're just very personable. And I have found that they really try their best to just hear people out. I mean, I've seen people faint in front of them. Grown men and women cry, people cry, and they were always really nice. They understood in their own way."

As for Ericha, she has one hope for the reunion show she'll be attending in Los Angeles: "I hope one day I can get a picture of Noel and Liam and me in the middle," she says. "That would really, really be great." Certainly better than a kick in the head.

# MAINE ROAD,
## Manchester,
## April 26–27, 1996

It feels safe to say that most of the people jostling for room in Manchester City's stadium, Maine Road, loved music and going to concerts. Even among that crowd, though, Luke Blackburn may have stood out. The Leeds local who currently lives in Malaysia has been to over one thousand gigs in his life and it all started at Maine Road.

"Music's quite a big passion for me," Luke understates. His love of Oasis started at "Hello," the opening track of *(What's the Story) Morning Glory?*, which he heard on the radio at fourteen. Using the money from his paper route, he bought the album. "CDs were quite expensive back in those days, at least ten pounds," he remembers. "So it was almost a week's worth of work." It was worth it, though, and he quickly saved up to buy the Oasis singles packaged to look like cigarette boxes, which flipped open to reveal the CDs inside, and then he bought *Definitely Maybe*.

When he heard that Oasis was making a hometown appearance at their beloved football team's stadium, Luke knew he wanted to go and, luckily, so did his mom. "My mom was always very supportive with my love of music, and she went to gigs a lot," he explains. "So she actually came along, too. It ended up with my mom and her friend, and then me and three of my friends. We got this deal, because in the old days, there used to be companies in Leeds that would sell a package of a coach trip and a concert. There was a tiny office with a blackboard outside that had all the concerts listed, and you just go up and pay your money, and you get this voucher and go."

Luke remembers turning up the morning of the gig to catch a ride and seeing sixteen single-decker yellow-and-black buses in a row all ready to take fans from Leeds to Manchester. "The queues were of mainly thirty-four-year-old lads, and then us," says Luke. "And it was so loud the whole way there and it took forever. Just this mass convoy of buses from Leeds heading over to Maine Road." Upon arrival, the stadium itself didn't particularly excite Luke: "It was just a stadium plunked in the middle of a housing estate," he recalls. But once inside he was thrilled to be there.

"We were just super buzzing about being at the show," he recalls. "I remember hearing Manic Street Preachers playing, and they were, like, one of my favorite bands at the time. And it was a good, good, solid support lineup with Ocean Colour Scene as well. We just sat on the seats watching the support bands, and when it was time for Oasis, we got up as close to the front as possible. But my mom— she's always a bit of a blagger—she and her friend went down to the front. And at the early shows, they had this semicircle area at the front where they would always put the first few keen fans. She went up to the security guards there and was like, 'Oh, I'm looking for my fourteen-year-old boy and his friends. We've lost them. Can we have a look in here to find them?' So she had managed to blag her way into the front section, and we didn't even know about this till afterwards," he says, laughing. Luke's experience was a little different. "I just remember being, like, a teenager surrounded by really old men." He didn't mind, though, because as soon as the first song came on everyone was pogoing. "I just remember jumping up and down the whole time and singing along, and we had to link arms to stay together, because it was pretty rowdy," he says. "It was pretty amazing to experience that, because we were left on our own the whole night. We just met my mum and her friend back at the coach after the show. I remember the liberating feeling of being on your own at fourteen, just in a massive field full of people just having a good time and singing."

The only disappointment about the night was this: "When they released the VHS cassette of the concert, it was of the night we weren't there," he says. "That was the only downside to it."

He later went to see them at Leeds Festival as well. "It was in 2000 and just after they released *Standing on the Shoulder of Giants*," he says. "But I remember being quite happy as a fan, because most of the songs they played were from the first two albums. I would have been eighteen or nineteen, and I ended up climbing up a tree to get a better view. So I was watching the set from this tree next to an ice cream van with a perfect view of the stage. I was just sat on this tree, singing along for every song. It was a good show."

Those two shows helped inspire a lifelong love of music and concerts in Luke, some of which he documents on social media. He kept going to gig after gig after gig, until suddenly he was at 999. There was only one real option for his one-thousandth show. "Liam Gallagher played at Leeds Festival that summer, doing the *Definitely Maybe* tour, and I took my mum to see that, so it was just like a perfect full-circle moment, because Mum took me to see them the first time," he says. "So we got to see that together at Leeds festival, for my one-thousandth concert."

# KNEBWORTH PARK,
## Stevenage, U.K.,
## August 10–11, 1996

It's hard to overstate how big the Knebworth concerts were both for Oasis and the fans. The two shows were held back-to-back at Knebworth Park, an estate in Hertfordshire, England. They were the biggest gigs of their era and quite the accomplishment for a band who was playing the back rooms in pubs just two years earlier. Something like one in twenty Brits tried to get tickets for the show and the guest list reportedly had seven thousand people on it. Eventually some 250,000 people—a record-setting number—managed to make it through the gates to pile into the park to see the musical event of the Britpop era. The Charlatans, Manic Street Preachers, the Prodigy, Cast, the Chemical Brothers, and Kula Shaker opened the shows, warming up the crowd for Liam, Noel, Bonehead, Guigsy, and Alan White to take the stage. It was hard to argue with Noel's reasoning when he strode onstage and declared: "You're making history, you lot." The shows were such smashes that at least one person thought the band should have broken up right after reaching that particular pinnacle. Guitarist Paul "Bonehead" Arthurs told *The Guardian* some years later, "I always thought we should have bowed out after the second night at Knebworth." The fans undoubtedly disagree.

————————

Devinder Bains is a little worried about telling this story. You see, her parents never knew that the school trip she went on in high school—the one where the bus broke down and she was nine hours late coming home—was all a lie. She was actually at Knebworth Park seeing Oasis.

Devinder grew up in Wolverhampton and had fallen in love with the band's sound straight away. "I really loved music growing up. My parents, they liked music, but they like Indian music, you know? And my older sister was kind of into this grunge sound, but then I found Oasis and it resonated. I liked their—excuse my language—their fuck-you attitude, to be honest. It was something that I wasn't really allowed to have. I liked their rebellious streak as well," she says. After seeing them perform on *Top of the Pops*, she also fell in love with their look and, like many other fans, very quickly started dressing like them. "Now that I've had time to sit with it, dressing like them was quite normal, if you were like a white lad growing up up north or in the Midlands. But as a little brown girl with really long hair often just tied back in a long ponytail? To be wandering around in bucket hats and Adidas jackets and the whole head-to-toe Adidas thing? It was quite weird, I'm sure, for people, but I really liked their style." Devinder had started working a part-time job at Burger King, using her earnings to buy Adidas clothes and whatnot from charity shops and to start saving up to buy tickets to see Oasis live.

The first show she went to was at the Civic Hall in Wolverhampton and she was smitten. "From then I just tried to get to every gig, usually in Birmingham at that point," she says. "In those early days, my parents weren't really happy about me going to concerts, so I would just lie and say I was going to the theater on a school trip to get out of the house, and then I'd come home with, like, a giant Oasis poster and they never really said anything," Devinder recalls, laughing. "I think they kind of knew, as there'd be a massive Oasis poster in my bedroom all of a sudden; it's come from nowhere, from a theater trip."

When Devinder learned about the Knebworth show, she knew she had to be there, but she had to work and couldn't wake up at 4 a.m. to queue for tickets. Years before Taskrabbit or other gig-work-for-hire companies existed, she came up with a clever solution. "I paid my sister, my younger sister, to stand in a queue outside our local Mike Lloyd [record] shop to get the tickets," she says. "She stood there with her friend from five or six a.m., and then me and my friend Katherine joined her on our way to work, I think about nine a.m., and just jumped in the queue, where she was quite near the front, bless her. Then off she went, and we got our tickets. To be fair, if I was a better sister, I could have got four tickets and got her and her friend one, but we just got them for me and Katherine. But we had our tickets and we ran around the whole of the queue. We were such dicks. We ran around the whole line of people still queuing, waving our tickets because we were so excited, and you know what? There are some things I'll never forget, even though my memory is awful, and I'll never forget us laughing in our Burger King uniforms, running around this whole queue of people who still didn't have their tickets, and just laughing all the way to work and just being so excited."

The only problem was that Devinder had to figure out how to get to Knebworth, which was over one hundred miles away, and what to tell her parents so she could do it. At first she tried a straightforward approach: "I asked them if I could go, and they said, no." Luckily she had a backup plan. "I just waited a couple of months, because we had got the tickets quite far in advance," she explains. "So like a month before, I told them that it was a school trip, and they were like, 'Of course, that's fine.' And so off I went, in my Adidas jacket from the charity shop, and I think brown flared cords and a pair of Adidas trainers that I got from the charity shop as well, and a bucket hat. And I borrowed some binoculars from a guy at work, which I lost."

She and her coworker and fellow Oasis fan, Katherine, boarded a bus and headed to Knebworth. "We were just kids. We didn't drink and we didn't take any food with us. We'd never been to anything like a big gig like this before," says Devinder, who now works as a journalist. "But we just ran in and we got to the front, not the really front bit, but the second front bit, and we just stayed there all day. It was just incredible. It is still probably one of the best gigs I've been to. The lineup was crazy, it was like the Chemical Brothers and the Prodigy, and we knew all the words to all the songs, like pretty much all day, to all the bands. I was there with my best mate, just having the best day, and we were just so out of place—a little Indian girl and a little Black girl with all these blokes drinking beers and bucket hats and stuff, and we just didn't care. We were just basically having the best day. And then Oasis came on and it was brilliant and I just knew then that it was going to be a seminal moment in music history. And I was just so lucky to be there."

There was one small dark spot on the otherwise perfect day,

though. "On the way back, all the coaches got stuck in the car park," says Devinder. "We were stuck in the car park for nine hours, and I just knew that my parents would be like, 'Where is she on the school trip?' And then I remember getting home at like, god, it must have been like eight in the morning, and I had my giant Oasis poster, I'd lost my jacket, just a T-shirt on, and they had waited up all night for me. And I was like, 'I'm really sorry, the coach got stuck,' and they were like, 'It's fine, don't worry about it.' I think they were just glad I wasn't dead, to be honest. I just remember knocking on the door and my dad answering and my mom asleep on the sofa downstairs, and I felt so guilty for about a minute, and then I was like, 'This was the best gig ever.'"

———

Rob Fiddaman had made a deal. His friends had tickets to see Oasis at Knebworth and he could have one, but he had to drive. "I hadn't been driving very long, but the deal was, I had to drive," he explains. "I was down in Norfolk and, you know, at the time, I hadn't really driven many miles out of where I lived, so it was quite a journey." It was a long trip for a new driver, but worth it for the Oasis fan. "It was my first proper gig; actually, my first festival," he says. "And what a moment to be there." The effort was worthwhile, not only because he got to see one of his favorite bands at one of their seminal performances, but because Oasis ended up helping shape the course of his life. You see, Rob now is a preeminent seller and evaluator of Oasis and Britpop memorabilia who has worked with a few memorable folks—Alan White, Tony McCarroll, Andy Bell, and Bonehead.

"I'd always been a big fan of the sixties and used to collect sixties memorabilia, and I was lucky enough to have a record signed by the Beatles, which was authenticated. It was the real deal," Rob says. "And I thought it was funny, no one was selling anything Oasis related. So I set up a website called the Britpop store, and I started selling Oasis memorabilia online, not a lot, just a few bits and pieces. Then [Oasis label boss] Alan McGee got in touch with me and said, 'You're either fucking mad or a genius.' He said, 'I want you to come down to my house and sell some things for my charity.'" And that's how it started.

Since then, Rob has slowly amassed an impressive collection of Oasis memorabilia (Alan White's snare drum, a few of Liam's tambourines, Alan McGee's gold disc for *Definitely Maybe*). He has also helped facilitate sales for an incredible array of items, ranging from the standard (gold records) to the obscure (the hat the clown wore in the "Wonderwall" video) to the impressive (Bonehead's scooter used in promo shots for their Earls Court show). One of the most memorable items he helped sell was Tony McCarroll's drum kit. "I'd met Tony, and I went to his house, and he had it in a cupboard, believe it or not, all stacked up, and he opened the door and a drumstick fell on the floor, and I picked it up and I tapped the drum. He said, 'Oh, that's the first time that's been played in, like, twenty-five years,'" says Rob. "He let me keep the drumstick, and he signed it. And I'd arranged somebody—I think it was Christie's or Bonhams, I can't recall now—but they came to look at the drum kit, and the woman from Christie's was like, 'Oh, these will go for about twelve hundred to fifteen hundred pounds.' I said, 'No, they're gonna go for about twenty-five hundred.' And they went for exactly what I said."

It was that strong sense of worth that helped Rob develop a reputation as an expert on valuing Britpop memorabilia. Shows including

Channel 4's *Posh Pawn*, the History Channel's *Pawn Stars U.K.*, and the Discovery Channel's *British Treasure, American Gold* have all had Rob on as an expert to help value items. Perhaps most notably, the band's management team asked him to help value Oasis memorabilia for the 2014 Oasis exhibition, *Chasing the Sun*, which displayed some of the instruments played on their first few albums, as well as vintage merchandise and rare, early photographs and footage of the group.

Rob, who also works as a DJ, spinning Britpop, of course, recognizes that it all started with those lads from Manchester. "If Oasis hadn't come along, I wouldn't have been writing for a regional paper, I wouldn't have been doing three radio shows a week. I wouldn't have done over one hundred appearances on the BBC and BBC TV. I wouldn't have done a BBC Britpop show. I wouldn't have written a book," he says. "They've really changed my life, haven't they? Without sounding cliché, but without them, I wouldn't have been doing all of this."

———

While many Knebworth attendees spent hours on the phone trying to get tickets to the massive concert, and many others have stark memories of being stuck in the car park for hours trying to get home after the gig, Anthony Lanni had no such problem. He doesn't even remember how he got the tickets as a fifteen-year-old, but once he had them, he simply walked to the gig, as it wasn't too far from home. "It was just the best day, really," he says. Anthony was such a fan of the band that he showed up on Liam Gallagher's doorstep a few months later and asked him for one of the platinum discs hanging on his wall.

"One of our friends kind of knew where Liam lived in London, so we thought as random, bored teenagers to just go down to London and see if we can see him," he says. "So we traveled off down to London, to St. John's Wood. We went to his house, it was like a town house and we were standing outside, and we weren't sure what to do next. So being a cheeky chap, I went and knocked on his door. He answered the door, and he wasn't best pleased, shall we say. He said, 'Don't knock on my door,' and told me to kind of go, really, and I went downstairs a little bit deflated." Being bored teenagers with nothing better to do, they continued loitering outside for half an hour or so, when Liam popped up in the window and appeared to be trying to get their attention. "He came to the window and was gesticulating with his hands, almost like with two fingers. And he opened the door and asked if any of us had a cigarette. So my friend went to hand him the cigarette. His hand was shaking. It was hilarious. Then Liam had a cigarette, and we were just talking for a while in his doorway, which is pretty amazing. He's a big Man City fan, and I was taking the mick out of that. He was showing us his Vespas. Behind him in his hallway were all these platinum and gold discs. Again, being the cheeky chap that I am, I said, 'Liam, let's have one of those discs.' And he kind of looked behind on the wall, then looked at me a bit funny, and then he turned around and picked one of these discs up off the wall and gave it to me. At this point, I was really shocked. I just thought, 'Okay, he was gonna let me look at it.' Then he said, 'There you go. If you don't ask, you don't get,' and I was like, 'What the actual F?' I just couldn't believe it.

"Liam went back inside and closed the door and I was a fifteen-year-old kid stuck in London with his platinum disc for *(What's the Story) Morning Glory?* So I went to a shop down the road. I got a load of newspapers and started to just wrap this thing up, because I'm in Central London. Like, how am I getting this home? As I was in the newsagent, someone came running into the shop and said, 'Liam just came out, and he was saying, "Where's ginger?"' Because I used to have really ginger hair. And Liam was saying, 'Where's ginger? Where's ginger?' And he told me to come back and knock on the door. I was like, 'Oh, he's gonna ask for it back.' So I went back to the house, knocked on the door, and by this point, there's quite a few people outside, more than our group, and I knocked on the door, and he actually let me in the house, and his, I think, girlfriend at the time, Patsy Kensit, was also there. He put his arm around me, was like, 'I've done this nice thing for you, so don't sell it.' I said, 'Of course, I'll never sell it.' And we chatted for a while. It was pretty amazing. Then he opened the door to let me out. It's hilarious. I felt like a celebrity at that point. It was just loads of people there taking photos and stuff. And then my friends started asking for stuff, and he gave my friend Paul a hole punch from his desk. And he also gave my friend Ricky a picture from his desk as well; I think it was him on a Vespa or something. So we went to make our way home, and stopped at McDonald's, and I remember sitting down with this thing on my lap; I wasn't going to let it out of my sight. When I got home and told my parents, and my dad, I don't think he believed me. It took him a while to kind of believe me. He thought I'd done something untoward."

Anthony was quite pleased with his cheeky coup, but when he saw a newspaper headline about Liam giving a fan a pair of sunglasses, he realized he was sitting on a story. "I rang up this number for *The Sun* newspaper and I went off and told him the story, and the guy was like, 'No, I don't believe you.' I was like, 'No, honestly.' Then *News of the World* came round on a Sunday, then *Daily Mail* came round. Then ITV News contacted me and I was on the news. I think I was mentioned quite a bit on MTV, and a few other bits and pieces like that. And I was known around locally as Oasis boy, and honestly, like twenty-five years on, people still ask me, 'You still got that platinum disc?'"

While Anthony promised Liam he would never sell the plaque, he started to have second thoughts when he couldn't get tickets for the reunion show. "I was devastated. Me and all my school friends who were big, staunch Oasis fans struggled," he says. Then he had an idea. He reached back out to the press and told them that he was trying to contact Liam to make an offer he hopefully couldn't refuse. "I wanted to reach Liam, saying that I'll give him the disc back for some tickets to the Oasis concert," he says. "In reality, I'm never going to do that, but it was just a tactic to try and get some tickets."

He never heard back from Liam.

# PÁIRC UÍ CHAOIMH,
## Cork, Ireland,
## August 14–15, 1996

When Sarah Breen was fifteen, or maybe sixteen, she came up with a genius plan to get the guys in Oasis to notice her—she was going to write a letter to their mom.

"I really wanted to meet Liam and, like, have him fall in love with me, ideally, or just be my friend. I thought we could be, like, really good friends," she says, laughing at the memory. "I was very keen to make contact. So when I was about fifteen, I wrote a letter to Peggy [Gallagher]. I gleaned their address from various different sources, there'd be a picture of them outside the house they grew up in, and the number would be visible. And then I read somewhere else the name of the street, and then the name of the area, so I was able to kind of glean what their address was, or what their mom's address was. Then I needed the postcode, because I knew that he couldn't send a letter to England without the postcode. So I rang, I don't know what, Royal Mail or Post or whatever it was, and I was like, 'I'm looking for a postcode for this house number.' And I read it out, and the guy said, 'Oh, this is the Oasis Gallaghers.' So obviously it wasn't the first time someone had asked for the postcode. So I sent a letter to Peggy, just saying, mostly, I just want to meet your sons and I love their songs and their music changed my life and blah blah. I heard nothing back for a while. And then a couple of months later, I was down at my nana's house, and my mother rang me, and she said, 'There's a letter here for you, and the postmark is Manchester.' And at that time, I just thought Manchester was like . . . it was like Mecca to me. So I ran home, and with shaking hands I opened the envelope. It was one of those big square A4 ones that said, 'Do Not Bend.' And there was a photograph of the band, and on the back of it, it said 'To Sarah, best wishes, Noel Gallagher,' and then 'Liam.' I was very pleased with myself. I remember bringing it to school and people going, 'Oh, you are so annoying.' I was like, 'Yeah, well, tell that to my good friends, Liam and Noel.'"

Sarah had fallen hard for the band as a kid. "I'm an only child. I have no older siblings, so I had nobody to kind of influence my music taste and I'm uncool," she says. "I know that I certainly didn't come to Oasis early. When *Definitely Maybe* came out, I would have been twelve, and by the time I was fourteen, I was absolutely, truly, one hundred percent obsessed. There wasn't one exact moment, but it was just a slow decline into obsession." By obsessed she means she had plastered her tiny little bedroom with every tabloid mention of Oasis, and in those days there were *a lot* of tabloid mentions. "There would be something for me in the paper every day, like, they get a haircut, or they would have been seen fighting in a pub or something like that," she says.

Sarah was desperate to see them live, but she lived in a very small rural village in Ireland and there was no way Oasis was coming through. However, riding high on the success of 1995's *(What's the Story) Morning Glory?* and their smash shows at Knebworth, Oasis was coming to Cork, Ireland, for two shows. "But I live very far away from Cork, and I would have been fourteen at the time, so the chances of me going to that concert would have been very slim, until my two older cousins, who were sisters, agreed to bring me, and I was able to secure a ticket, and that was the first time I saw Oasis live," she says. "I think it's fair to say my life was kind of changed by this." Sarah and her two cousins took a coach to Cork. "I remember arriving, and there just being buses and people everywhere, but, like, people wearing Oasis T-shirts and boys with the cool haircuts. And I just thought, 'Oh my god, this is heaven,'" she says. She and her cousins got off the coach and went straight to a pub, where Sarah got an alcopop or two ("It was my first time being tipsy!") before heading to the show. "We ran into some people leaving the pit and we ended up buying their plastic wristbands from them for, like, ten pounds each or something," she says. "The guys tore them off and then we stuck them onto our wrists and held them together with chewing gum and used them to get into the pit, which I thought was pretty genius. I'd do it again today."

Sarah loved everything about the experience, but didn't get to see the band again until she moved to Dublin for college. It was 2003 and the band was touring in support of their 2002 album, *Heathen Chemistry.* At that point, Sarah's friends weren't quite as into Oasis as she was, so she went to the show alone. After queuing overnight to get her ticket from Ticketmaster, she made her way to the venue, Dublin's Point Theater, and camped out there for hours to make sure she got to the very front row. While she was in line, she overheard two guys talking about where the band was staying while they were in town for a few shows. At the concert, Sarah had a stroke of luck and almost caught Alan White's drumsticks as he threw them into the crowd. "They kind of went over my head," she says with a shrug. The near-catch would be important later.

The next day she and her friend Connor went to go stake out the hotel in hopes of meeting the band. "We were waiting, waiting, waiting," she says, much to the chagrin of the doorman, who was unsuccessfully urging them to move along. Finally, something happened: "This guy who we had seen go in and out a couple of times with an Oasis haircut came over to us and was like, 'Hey, are you waiting to see Oasis?' We said, 'Yeah.' And he was like, 'Okay, come up here for a second.'" They followed him around the building, where he told them a story. "Right, I'm traveling with the band, but I have these bootleg CDs that I want Liam to sign so I can sell them online. I obviously can't ask him to sign them, but he will sign them for a fan." He gave Sarah the CDs and said he'd come get her when Liam was in the lobby of the hotel. They waited a bit, and then he reappeared, gave a nod, and Sarah managed to slip past the doorman. "There's people milling around, and sitting on one of the couches with a guitar case beside him was Liam with his sunglasses on. I was like, 'Oh, Jesus Christ.' And so I just kind of walked in," Sarah says, laughing. "And I just said, 'Liam, is it okay if I sit down for a second?' And he says, 'Yeah, no problem.' So I sat down. I was thinking, 'Oh my god.'" Sarah was studying journalism and decided to not only get the CDs signed but also to get an exclusive quote for her college newspaper, and to snap a photo of them with her disposable camera. She managed to get all three done before the doorman spotted her. "He tapped me on the shoulder and said, 'Excuse me, are you staying in this hotel?' And he'd seen us outside for about eight hours, so I was like, 'No, I'm not,'" Sarah explains. "And then Liam said, 'It's okay. It's cool. She can stay.' And then the doorman said, 'Okay,' and then *he* had to leave."

Sarah and Connor stayed another minute and then headed outside to wait to see the rest of the band and get more pictures. "And then Alan White came out and I said, 'Hey, Alan, I almost got your drumsticks last night at the gig,'" she says. "And then I said, 'Any chance of tickets to the gig tonight?' And he was like, 'Sure, what's your name?' So then he wrote my name on his hand, and then Connor said, 'And me! And I'm gonna bring a friend!'

"We went to the venue later on, and it was the first time I'd ever gone to a venue with no ticket. And the security guard was like,

'Where's your ticket?' And I said, 'Oh, we're on the guest list.' And he was like, 'Okay, you know where to go?' And pointed us to a couple of different kiosks. And then somebody else asked, 'Which guest list are you on? Are you press? Are you with the promoter?' And then I said, 'I think we are on the Oasis list.'" Sure enough, handwritten on the top of the guest list was her name plus two. The small act of kindness to a fan just cemented her love for what was already her favorite band. "The world is a hundred and sixty-five million years old, or whatever it is, and I happened to cross paths with Oasis when I was thirteen or fourteen years old, ready to listen to some kind of life-changing music. I do feel very lucky that we had that intersection, and it definitely came at the right time for me."

# ROSEMONT HORIZON,
## Chicago,
## August 27, 1996

There is no denying that the touring schedule that Oasis followed was absolutely brutal. They had been on the road for most of 1994, 1995, and 1996. A steady stream of hotel rooms, traveling, gig after gig, night after night, for three years. The few breaks they did have usually meant being in the studio, a.k.a. more work and more time together. It would be a lot for anyone and particularly a lot for two famously tetchy brothers. Noel had already split from the band once, leaving for San Francisco after their show at Hollywood's Whisky a Go Go went badly. At the end of 1996, after another two years on the road, tensions between the brothers reportedly reached another breaking point.

At the time, their record label, Creation, told *Melody Maker* that the band had "internal differences." There may have been some lingering bad feelings over the fact that Liam had bailed on the tour before it even started. Instead of going to the airport to star the tour, Liam was house hunting. He had apparently decided to stay in the

U.K. because he had sold his house and needed to find a new one, determined to come home from the tour to a house and not be forced to stay in another hotel room. Since Liam wasn't there, Noel had to front the band until Liam joined the tour three or so days later. The result was that Noel had to take over singing duties during the first few stops on their U.S. tour. James Deia was at the one in Chicago at Rosemont Horizon.

James had already seen Oasis a few times. "They were actually my first concert," he says. "There is a radio station called Q101 here in Chicago, and they would throw, like, a mini little festival with bands called Twisted Xmas. And Oasis played it in late '95." He saw them again at the Aragon Ballroom for a headlining gig in 1996, and even went to a *Be Here Now* listening party at the Metro in Chicago, where fans gathered at the venue to hear the album. "Talk about a dated concept," he says, laughing. "A bunch of strangers standing in silence in a half-sold Metro club listening to the new album."

So he was a seasoned fan when, at thirteen or fourteen years old, he headed to Rosemont Horizon to see Oasis, except Liam never appeared onstage, and instead Noel took over on the mic. "It was kind of surreal. You felt like you were seeing a divorce in real time," he says. These days, if one of the Gallagher brothers can't or won't perform, James could step in, because he plays guitar in Chicago's premiere Oasis cover band, Broasis, covering the band's greatest tunes. (More on that a few chapters ahead.)

At the time, though, he was a little befuddled by what he was seeing on stage at the Rosemont. "I understood the dynamic of, like, 'Oh well, they're Noel's songs.' He wrote them, so he has the confidence to deliver them. I liked it. I didn't enjoy it more or less. It was hard to understand the gravity of it at that time. And I think shortly after that, they just canceled the whole tour and flew back to England.

"There's interviews out there where Noel's, like, 'We should have taken a year off,' but they went right back in and made the third record and then toured, and then the drugs are taking over, and that's when the fighting was the big thing. I don't know what this fight was about, but Liam wasn't there," James says.

CANCELED

## CHARLOTTE HORNETS
## TRAINING CENTER,
### Charlotte, North Carolina,
### September 12, 1996

Liam skipping the first few tour dates to buy a house wasn't the only point of strife with the brothers. There were also rumors that Noel and Liam were still fighting with each other over the band's performance on the TV series *MTV Unplugged*. The partially acoustic show took place August 23, 1996, at Royal Festival Hall in London. In a documentary about the famed MTV series, Noel said that over the course of the two-week rehearsals for the gig, Liam had "only turned up once or twice." Producers said that Liam claimed he had a sore throat and would walk out of rehearsals, letting Noel take over the vocals. When the day of the performance came, Liam reportedly showed up just an hour before the band was due to go on and was completely shit-faced, according to Noel. Producers weren't sure whether to put on a massive recorded performance without the band's lead singer or to cancel the whole gig. In the end, Noel did it. "Liam ain't gonna be with us tonight 'cause he's got a sore throat," Noel said as he walked onstage, sat on a tall stool, and picked up his acoustic guitar. "So you're stuck with the ugly four." The resulting performance was not what the producers had in mind, but it was mesmerizing and commanding as Noel sang the words he had written. In the documentary, Noel patted himself on the back: "I think I did a fucking great job to be quite honest with you." Liam reportedly sat in the audience and heckled.

The story is that Noel was still frustrated with Liam over that performance and that boiled over into a fight somewhere between New York and North Carolina and Noel bolted back to the U.K.

Whatever the exact cause of the rift, the result was that, in mid-September 1996, Oasis abruptly called off its tour. The cancellation meant the band would be on a much-needed break through the end of 1996. However, for the fans that meant the band was cutting short a three-week American tour with five dates to go, including a show in Charlotte, North Carolina. Mike Dugan had a front-row seat to some of the action.

"In 1996 I was a freshman at a small college in North Carolina. Like most first-year students, I was looking for things to participate in and fill up my time. I was peripherally involved with my high school newspaper, so I decided to see if I could help out and get some more writing experience. Apparently they were so starved for content and writers they let me review a CD I bought in Ireland that summer by a band no one in central NC had ever heard of: Manic Street Preachers," says Mike. "The review was terrible and definitely had typos as well as literal band member descriptions from the liner notes. In addition to the school paper, I also joined the college radio station, hoping I would one day get my own show to play all of my Brit rock bands that I didn't hear anywhere else but my CD player (which I did!). When the music director, Mike F., found out I wrote the review, he told me a record label rep offered tickets to see the Manics and Screaming Trees open for Oasis in Charlotte, and we could interview James Dean Bradfield from the Manics before the show. I just about lost my mind! I was less than a month into my first year of college and I was already getting free concert tickets and would meet the band and then some." Mike D. and Mike F. agreed to do the interview and go to the show together.

"The day of the show we make the two-hour drive down to what I think was called Charlotte Coliseum in the 1990s. We were told to get there pretty early so we could have time before the show to talk to James. We waited outside with probably a few thousand kids waiting to get in . . . and we waited . . . and waited . . . and waited. Finally the rep comes out to find us. I don't remember how, since neither of us had cell phones. Anyways, she tells us we need to go to a hotel to interview James. We ask if we will still be able to get back in time to see the show, and she says there isn't going to be a show and they are about to break that news to the thousands of waiting fans, so we better get out of there ASAP," he recalls.

They headed to the hotel, and soon Mike D. was nervously interviewing James Dean Bradfield in his hotel room. "It probably lasted less than twenty minutes, but felt like an hour or two," he says. James ended up walking the two Mikes to the lobby, where they run into Oasis drummer Alan White. "James introduces us and we shake hands. We continue to the hotel bar and stand at the end. James orders a round of drinks for himself, a few other people with him, and I'm pretty sure something showed up in front of me," remembers Mike. "All of a sudden there is a lot of commotion down at the other end of the bar, hooting and hollering, and maybe a barmaid—no joke—lifting her skirt up to the crowd she was attending to." That's when he spots Bonehead, who spots James standing next to Mike and comes to join their group. "The next thing I know, a familiar figure saunters up behind us and I can peripherally see from my seat at the bar that this person is playing with Mike F.'s backwards Kangol cap, by picking it up and dropping it on his head over and over for what felt like five minutes. It was, of course, Liam. I don't think we were officially introduced, as we were all sort of chatting with James and Bonehead; it was loud and Liam was otherwise occupied.

"After all the ruckus, it seems that Oasis were leaving right then," Mike recalls. "They were leaving the bar and walking straight out to their tour bus. Liam is still chatting with the barmaids, I think, all the way out to the tour bus. We, of course, had to leave, too. Later on we find out Noel had already left for the U.K. either earlier that day or the day before and they were canceling the rest of that leg of the U.S. tour."

Johnny Hopkins, the press relations agent for Creation Records at the time, does remember that particular tour, but didn't think too much of it when it was happening. "That was a turbulent tour. Though most tours by most bands are," he says. "Despite the abrupt end to that tour it never seemed likely that they would split at that point. Of course, Oasis went on to survive several more turbulent tours."

The band needed a break from the road and they needed to record their third album in the hopes of matching the success of *(What's the Story) Morning Glory?*

# EARLS COURT,
## London,
## September 25–27, 1997

After their tumultuous U.S. tour, the band went to the studio to record their third album, *Be Here Now*, between 1996 and '97. Noel frequently claimed he had written the band's first three albums before *Definitely Maybe* came out, so when he and Oasis producer Owen Morris decamped to the Caribbean island of Mustique to record the demos, he had the songs ready to go. With the demos in hand, the whole band headed to London's legendary Abbey Road Studios to start recording in the shadow of the Beatles. The media circus became too much, though, and the band decamped to Ridge Farm in Surrey to work there, but they still couldn't finish the album. They then returned to London, eventually finishing their third album. *Be Here Now* was released on August 21, 1997, and sold four hundred thousand copies on the first day in the U.K. alone. With the album complete, the band was headed back on the road, including another stop at Earls Court in London, and the fans were ready for another round of shows.

———

Lindsay Melbourne was hungry. She didn't mind, though, because she had the Oasis singles. "I started saving my dinner money up from school every week, and I used it to buy the back catalog of Oasis singles," she explains. "There must have been maybe ten singles. There was everything from *Definitely Maybe*, everything from *What's the Story*, other singles; and they all had free B-sides on them, so you'd get four tracks per single. So I'd save my dinner money each week. I'd go to the one record shop in Stevenage and I would buy that CD."

When *Be Here Now* came out in August 1997, she skipped breakfast, too. "I went and queued, I think it came out on a Saturday, so I was there at, I don't know, six in the morning," she says. "I wanted to make sure I was one of the very first people to hear that record, before anybody else. That was my reason for going." She rushed home with the album and played it on the little CD player in the bedroom she shared with her brother. "They used to sell these Oasis fan magazines at the news agent. I don't know who wrote these magazines, but there were just loads of Oasis magazines, so I plastered my entire bedroom, like ceiling and walls, with just Liam and Noel everywhere. I would just go home and listen to Oasis. I also really vividly remember a mini-disc player. So I think maybe at some point I transferred it all to a mini disc.

"As soon as I found Oasis, that was it. They were the entire world. They were my entire personality. They pretty much still are," she says, laughing. Lindsay's fandom started young. Her mother had her at seventeen and she grew up hearing music all the time. She didn't have a particularly easy home life and Oasis quickly became more than just music—the band an escape and a lifeline. "Oasis gave me something to hold on to," she says. "I didn't have many friends at school. We moved around a lot. My mum married someone else. We left Liverpool, came to London, went to Hertfordshire, so I went to secondary school, not knowing anybody. Never really found a clique of friends. Got bullied a lot. Oasis made me feel like I was just part of something. Like it didn't matter that I didn't have anything at school or any friends or any support from teachers. I had Oasis, and that was enough."

Oasis was there for her when not much else was. "Not to make it too traumatic, but [my parents] were alcoholics," Lindsay says. While sometimes school can be an escape from a bleak home life, that wasn't the case for Lindsay. "I had a birthday party at home, and I invited this bunch of girls from school. Well, they were the type of girls that would befriend you and then be really nasty to you as, like, a thing. I'd invited these girls around to my house, and I must have been about fifteen, and my mom made loads of food, like hot dogs. I remember that. And when I was out of the room, they squashed everything into the carpet. They squashed all the food into the carpet. They also all bought me, like, bath bombs and scents and things because they told me that I smelled. It was really awful," she recalls. "And I just remember them all going in. I don't even know why I invited them around. When I look back now, I'm so angry at myself for the whole thing, but I remember just going into my room and blasting *(What's the Story) Morning Glory?* Just blasting and blasting that. My little brother was really young at the time, like, three or four, and we were jumping around the front room to that and getting through that moment. It was really tough. It was really shit at school."

Even in her darkest hours, Oasis inspired her. They made her think bigger and better things were possible. "There was just a connection," she says. "Like people who don't grow up with much and going on and doing something big. They were just like me. They're from a northern town, went to a shit comprehensive school, got no support, people not telling you that you could achieve anything. Just being two lads from Manchester who go out and literally become the biggest band in the world. They just gave everybody the sense that you could do it, too."

It was through Oasis that she found her people. She had started working at a shop in town ("It was called Sport and Ski in a shitty shopping center in a place called Stevenage, where nothing happens") and made friends with a few guys who were really into music and started taking her to shows. One of the biggest disappointments of her life is that she missed seeing Oasis at Knebworth. It was particularly frustrating, because she basically lived there. "We lived so close to Knebworth that if there was a show at Knebworth, you could hear it in your back garden," she says. While at the time, she was too young to go to the show alone, she couldn't even hear the concert, because her family was out of town when Oasis played. "It was heartbreaking," she says.

When Oasis played Earls Court on the *Be Here Now* tour in September 1997, she was there. Her friend Kev from the sports shop got her a ticket and she went with him and his girlfriend. "It was just insane," she says. "Gigs are just not like that anymore. Just a sea of people from the front to the back. I just always imagine it as like being in the sea, just being caught in a wave, just being carried around by the crowd. I remember the Verve supporting and Richard Ashcroft coming out onstage and being able to see the Levi's tab on the back of his jeans, and being like, 'Shit, they're actually on the stage in front of me.' When Liam and Noel came out, and it was through the phone box and all that, my mind was just absolutely blown that they were there in real life. Like, they're there and I'm in the same room as them, and they actually exist.

"I just went to loads of shows on my own for the rest of that tour. Went to Edinburgh, went to Cardiff, went to Manchester, I did three in Wembley," she says. She was sixteen years old and she was sleeping in train stations and following Oasis on tour and waiting for hours in the queue to be in the front row at the concerts.

When the *Be Here Now* tour did three nights at Wembley Arena, Lindsay was there. Every day. "For the Wembley shows, I got dropped off at six in the morning by my stepdad, who was traveling in. It was December. It was snowing. I waited for three days in a row. I was first in the queue at six a.m., and I was there for the entire day, in the snow, so I could be the first one in. I remember having bin bags tied around my feet because it was so cold," she says.

For her, it was all worth it. "I was first every day, or in the first, say, five or ten people. As soon as they open the doors, you just run. They let you through the gates, and you just run to the front of Wembley Arena. I got to the front, I had bruised ribs, because everything was a crush behind you, and you would just hold on for dear life. I don't remember eating. I remember being passed water, but never went to the toilet," she says. "But that moment that Liam came through the phone box, and I was what, like, twenty feet away? That gives me goose bumps, even just thinking about it now. It was incredible."

Whatever Lindsay went through as a teenage fan, freezing in the cold with trash bags tied to her feet or sleeping in the Edinburgh train station, was time well spent, in her mind. "It just gave me something to focus on, when everything else around me was so shit. Like, my home life was shit. Everything was awful," she says. "But those shows gave me moments of just pure ecstasy."

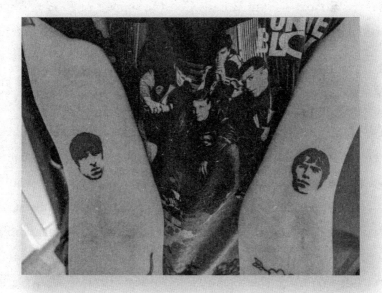

Lindsay Melbourne showing off
her Gallagher brother tattoos

Lindsay is now a happily married mom with a successful career and is firmly in what she calls her "healing era." She was able to come out the other side of a tough childhood, thanks in no small part to the music made by those two brothers from Burnage. "Oasis literally changed my entire life. They shaped my entire life," she says. "I worked shit jobs for years, but like, in the end, I played in bands. I've got Oasis photo books I looked at for years, and I always wanted to do that, and it took me a long time to get to that point, but I'm a music photographer now. I made a documentary about the band, Idles, too—and that's all because of them."

———

"That crowd was crazy," recalls Ben Wood. It was his first-ever concert and it was a doozy—Oasis at Earls Court in support of *Be Here Now*. He had just turned thirteen years old and his dad had brought him to the show, not expecting total mayhem.

Ben's dad loved music and he and his friends would travel all over to see shows, including Oasis. "I think they were at that one where Liam got his teeth knocked out in Germany," he says. When tickets for the Earls Court gig went on sale, his dad and his friends had a master plan. "They'd be at work, and then one of them would skive off and be on the Oasis ticket hotline," he explains. Eventually someone would get through and buy the tickets for the whole group. His dad would go to a lot of gigs, and occasionally he and his friends would say, "Let's take the kid along." Ben was a big Oasis fan already, having asked for *Definitely Maybe* for Christmas (it was his very first CD), so when he heard he was going to the Earls Court show, he went "berserk." His dad may have had some doubts about bringing his kid with him when he saw the crowd, though. "We were stood next to a guy. My dad was like, 'Look,' and I looked down and this guy's rolling an absolutely massive spliff," Ben recalls, laughing. "I'll be honest, though, it was exciting. It was carnage. It was like Gomorrah in there."

Things went up- or downhill depending on your perspective once the music started. "I've been in a few heavy mosh pits in my time, but that was raucous. It was really raucous. There was a lot of beer happening. There was a lot of weed smoking. The Manchester lot had come down to London in the bucket hats, and they were pretty excitable," says Ben, who knows gigs, as he is the frontman of Ben Wood & the Bad Ideas.

"My dad said to me, 'Look, it's pretty heavy here, kid.' I was a big lad, but he said, 'If you get stuck in here, just go to the front and they'll pull you out, and you can just run off through the aisle to the side.'" Ben heeded the warning, but his dad did not. "Ten minutes later, I've lost him. I look over, and him and his mates are getting cooked up at the front and getting pulled out. And bless his heart, you know, I think this was his last foray into rock and roll." Ben pauses a moment. "I think, in honesty, that maybe they just wanted a beer."

Despite the fact that Ben was a big kid and wearing a red Oasis T-shirt from the Knebworth show (which he'd bought at an Our Price shop in Colchester; "I still wear it to work some days in the studio," he says), his dad didn't find him for a while during the gig. For his part, Ben was content to just watch from the relative safety of the sidelines, watching the chaos, the lasses, and of course the music. He loved the Verve, but Oasis was something else. "Oasis, they just floored everything. That wall of sound was absolutely enormous," Ben says. "I didn't have a lot of reference points then, but I do now, and hearing their sound in my head. They were just massive. They were absolutely colossal."

That first concert turned Ben's love for the band into a lifelong and committed relationship. "I've never known a band like them, or rather, I've never had a connection to a band like that," he says. "They were honest to who they were.

"Those songs unify people, and they're deep in our culture," he says. "They mean a lot to me."

A young Ben Wood playing guitar

# HAMMERSTEIN BALLROOM,
## New York City,
## October 7–8, 1997

Oasis were back in New York and had just heard four of the greatest words in the English language: "Ladies and gentlemen, Oasis." Those four little words were said by *Friends* star Matthew Perry, who was hosting *Saturday Night Live*, where Oasis was the musical guest, one of the biggest milestones for a band trying to make it in the States. Oasis played "Don't Go Away" and "Acquiesce" as the audience in Studio 8H looked on appreciatively. The next night the band played Hammerstein Ballroom in Midtown Manhattan.

When Liam Gallagher looked out into the crowd pushing against the stage at Hammerstein, he may have noticed a sixteen-year-old girl in a black Oasis shirt standing right in the center of the pit that had formed in front of him. That was Jennifer Huffman, who, in every teenage girl's dream, had her mom, dad, and two sisters with her to see her favorite band in the world. "They didn't want to send me into New York City by myself," she says. "So they're like, 'Okay, everybody gets a ticket.' Luckily back then, it was twenty-five dollars a ticket." So she dutifully stood in line outside the Ticketmaster, which was inside a video store on Long Island, to get tickets for the entire family. At Hammerstein, she insisted they get there early so she could be as close as possible to the stage for her first-ever Oasis gig.

Also at the show was Brian Zwolak, also wearing an Oasis shirt to his first-ever Oasis show. "I was going to see them at the Paramount Theater at Madison Square Garden, not the Garden itself, but the Theater at Madison Square Garden. My brother and I had tickets lined up to see them play, but they were in the last row, the last two seats," Zwolak explains. "And we said, 'No way our first experience is going to be that. We need to be right there.'" So instead, he and his brother got tickets to see them play at Hammerstein, where the general-admission entry policy allowed for being much closer to the band. He and his brother got there early and managed to push their way close to the front. Turns out his future wife was standing about five feet away.

That night at Hammerstein kicked off a massive, lifelong fandom for both Zwolak and now Mrs. Zwolak. Jennifer has seen the band forty-eight or forty-nine times. "I've lost track," she says. Brian thinks he's been at about forty-two or forty-three shows. "I'm always just a few shows behind," he says with a sigh. As such ardent fans, their paths crossed multiple times before they finally met, most notably at Radio City Music Hall in 2001. "It was the Brotherly Love Tour with Oasis and the Black Crowes," says Brian. "I was standing outside the side stage door, like the backstage door, with my brother. He and I got there early to try to meet the band. We were standing out there and my brother pointed out these two girls who were wearing these matching T-shirts and he's like, 'Oh, those girls are hardcore. They are major fans. They've got a tour blog and they've been traveling around following the band.' And I thought, 'Wow, that's cool,' and remember thinking, 'Oh, one of them's pretty cute.'" After the Hammerstein show cemented her love for the band, Jennifer had gone deep into fandom, starting a blog called *The Oasis Fan Guide*, where she documented her love of the Gallaghers and her adventures following the band on tour with her friend. She had already gone to seven or so Oasis shows by the time of the Radio City gig.

"My brother and I, we had good seats, we were like maybe tenth, twelfth row, center," says Brian. "I saw the two girls with the shirts and they were front row, going crazy, and Liam Gallagher came out and I guess dedicated a song to you?" He looks at Jennifer, who is sitting next to him.

"It was 'Slide Away,'" she helpfully supplies.

"Right, he dedicated 'Slide Away' to the two girls in the front and I was like, 'Oh wow, that's really pretty hardcore,'" Brian finishes. "Then my brother and I were back at Penn Station, getting on the train to head back to Long Island, and coming running past me was that girl in the Oasis T-shirt, and she got on the same train as I did. And then when the train pulled into our last stop, which that was the stop that I was getting off at, I saw the same girl in the Oasis T-shirt running off the train to her car. So I'm like, 'Oh, that's interesting, she must live somewhere around here.' And that's it. I didn't think too much of it. Fast-forward, maybe like a year later. I was on, believe it or not, a Yahoo! personals site. One day I received an email and it said, 'These people might be a match for you,' and I looked at the first picture and it was the girl in the Oasis T-shirt! So I clicked on it and I wrote her and said, 'Hey, by any chance were you at the Radio City musical show in 2001?' You wrote back yes," he says to Jennifer, "and, really, the rest is history. And two kids later, here we are." Their kids' names? Lyla and Noel, of course.

"The crazy thing was, we both had Oasis license plates," says Jennifer. "We had not known each other and we were basically living within a ten-mile radius of each other and had never seen each other."

"There's not too many people on Long Island driving around with Oasis plates," agrees Brian.

Once they started dating, they began going to Oasis shows together, including their first Madison Square Garden show. "The first time they played the actual Madison Square Garden, I think that would probably be my top show," says Jennifer. "I had been in the fifth row and I ran and gave Liam roses, 'cause he was 'in the Garden.'"

"I lifted her over the barricade to make sure that she gave them to Liam," adds Brian. "And then I guess it was maybe three or four songs later, he came out and he pointed directly at her and made sure that he gave his tambourine to her. As you can imagine, she was going nuts."

Jen points out that she actually has three tambourines from Liam, smiling as she adds, "They've always been good to me, I'll tell you that."

# WEMBLEY ARENA,
## London,
## December 16–18, 1997

In 1997 Oasis brought their *Be Here Now* tour to London's Wembley Arena, the smaller indoor venue near Wembley Stadium. They played for three nights, all in front of sold-out crowds. The concerts were both a victory lap for the band, playing one of London's largest venues after months on the road, and a holiday extravaganza that meant the band would actually have a few weeks off.

In the crowd was Lou Boyd. He had grown up near Heathrow Airport, hearing the Concorde take off overhead, so when he first heard the song "Supersonic," it resonated. "When you heard them using a word like 'supersonic,' well, that was in your kind of realm of experience, because you'd be hearing these Concordes breaking the sound barrier twice a day. So I just thought it was cool," he says.

He had a ticket to see them at Earls Court, but ended up giving it away, while he went on a "lads' holiday" to Italy. While there he crashed his moped, which he describes as "pretty Gallagher-esque behavior." Still, he was sad to miss the show, particularly as his twin brother had attended and had bragging rights about it. "The next time they came round, we were like, 'Right, we're going to do this.' We had to go to Wembley Arena, which is like the smaller version of Wembley Stadium, which is where they were playing. It used to be an industrial estate, and we went and queued up on a Friday night, because the tickets went on sale at eight a.m. Our group were fourteen or fifteen years old at the time, and we were just, 'Bye, Mum. I'll see you in twenty-four hours, hopefully.' There was a queue of already about a thousand people there. There were guys, like, off their nut. They were probably thinking, 'I need to get through this cold night. I'll just get wasted.' And it's a massive queue. Just thinking about, nowadays, how that wouldn't be allowed to happen. There was, like, one security guard, who would walk past the queue every hour, bored shitless. And the smell of skunk was just insane. We were taking shifts and going into this block of flats, like an apartment block, because it was heated, sleep for an hour, and then come back out. Then at eight o'clock, they let you into the ticket office. I just handed over cash. All night we had wads of cash, and then we got the tickets, and we just went home. Nowadays you'd be robbed. You'd either be robbed for the cash beforehand or you'd be robbed for the tickets on the way home. It was just absolutely mad. And this was still three or four months before the gig. But it was kind of bonding in a way. I've never worked harder physically for a ticket."

Months later, after all the hard work they went through to get the tickets, Lou and his friends finally headed to Wembley Arena to see Oasis play. "It was great. It was brilliant," he says. "They had a guy dressed like Santa and throwing out T-shirts, and I'm quite tall, I'm six foot four, and I jumped in the air to grab one and smashed a guy in the face with my elbow. Feel guilty about it still, but I caught it. Wore it all the time till basically it fell apart." It was a hard-won souvenir, which is why it is still his all-time favorite.

## PATRIOT CENTER,
### Fairfax, Virginia,
### January 9, 1998

After their three-night residency at Wembley Arena, Oasis headed back to the U.S. to play a string of shows across the country, and for a performance on *The Tonight Show with Jay Leno*, before heading to Asia. One of the early stops was at the Patriot Center on the campus of George Mason University.

Sarah Connolly had gone through a *lot* to make it to Fairfax, Virginia, in time to see Liam and Noel take the stage. She had fallen hard for Oasis after seeing one video on MTV and, like many other fans, she connected with their scrappy attitude, Beatles-inspired sound, and the bravado that convinced two working-class kids from Burnage that they could be the biggest band in the world. "TikTok would call them delulu these days," she says, laughing. She loved it all. When she saw that they were playing in the U.S. she knew she had to see them. However, as a devoted fan, she knew that just because an Oasis tour was booked didn't mean it would definitely happen. After all, U.S. fans had been burned several times before when band tensions resulted in canceled shows. So Sarah knew that she couldn't risk them breaking up before they got to Dallas, the closest tour stop.

She convinced her mother she had to see them early in the U.S. tour and it should probably be in Fairfax. Her single mother, who worked as a waitress in one of the local casinos, scraped together enough cash to buy her Oasis-obsessed daughter tickets to the show and the bus fare to get there. She didn't have any spending money to give her daughter, but then Reginald VelJohnson of *Family Matters* and *Die Hard* fame unintentionally stepped in to help by winning big at the casino and giving his waitress a hefty tip. She gave the money to her then sixteen-year-old, who trundled onto a Greyhound bus from Shreveport, Louisiana. Destination? Scranton, Pennsylvania, where she would meet a stranger from the internet—an online friend from an Oasis fan group—who would go to the show in Fairfax with her. Sarah, now a forty-three-year-old mother of three, cracks up laughing as she tells this story: "Can you imagine?" The story gets worse. In their infinite wisdom, the bus company had routed her from Shreveport to Atlanta, where she was robbed of half her money at gunpoint while standing outside the bus. After she was robbed, the cop said he could file a report, but she would most likely miss her bus if he did the paperwork, and there was no way she was missing her bus and possibly her only chance to see Oasis. She got onto the bus to New York's always delightful Port Authority ("I inadvertently got to see the World Trade Center; I poked my head out and saw it, so there was that," she recalls) and then another bus to Scranton and finally to Fairfax.

The show was amazing, of course, and they managed to meet the opening act, Cornershop, which was also amazing, but after the show was less so. "The problem was that when my mom booked the tickets,

she made sure that we had the Greyhound to get from Scranton to Fairfax and then back to Scranton. Down here in Shreveport, Greyhound
stations are open twenty-four hours, so even though our bus didn't technically run until like five in the morning, she figured we could just spend
the night at the bus station," Sarah explains. "Okay, cool, but there was
snow everywhere and it was freezing cold, and the bus station shut at
ten. So I ended up calling my mom, and explained that it was below
freezing and the station was closed. I had a great-aunt that worked in
Washington, D.C., at the time, so my mom called my aunt Virginia. My
aunt's like, 'Well, I can't be there for at least an hour or so,' and my mom's
like, 'Well, Sarah's going to freeze to death.' So she called the cops. Now,
this is before cell phones, so I didn't know any of this was happening,
so next thing you know, like six cop cars roll up to pick us up and I'm
like, 'Oh god, I'm going to die.' They picked us up and we waited at the
bus station until my aunt got there." Sarah made it back to Shreveport,
eventually, and immediately logged on to the internet to send a message
to the Whatever mailing list, recounting her adventures to hundreds of
other strangers on the internet, a.k.a. her fellow Oasis fans.

The Whatever mailing list was how Sarah met other fans, including the friend she connected with in Scranton for the concert. They
were all part of a large community of Oasis fans and music lovers who
found each other through online mailing lists in those early internet
days way before the age of social media, online mailing lists allowed
people to connect with each other and keep up on news about the
band. "You would send an email to [redacted email address] and then
it would go to everybody else in the mailing list," she explains. "It
could become very cluttered in your inbox." It sounds a bit like those
reply-all email wars, except everyone willingly signed up for them.

Sarah had learned about the Whatever mailing list when she was flipping through *Spin* magazine and read that Oasis had a website. Sarah didn't have a way to actually get onto the web. "Nobody had a computer here because I'm in, you know, Hicksville," she explains. "So we had gone to Dallas and gone to a Circuit City, and they had computers where you could test-drive the internet, and I was like, 'Yes!' This was months later, but I remembered the address and I typed in www.oasisinet.com. I sat there and I waited, and nothing happened. And I tried it again. I didn't know back then, of course, that you had to put the 'http' in front of it. I didn't know. So after, like, twenty minutes, my mom was like, 'Okay, you can't just stand at the computer.' But I was like, 'It's Noel and it's Liam!' But I had to come home. Then that year for Christmas, I got WebTV, and I finally went on the band's website, and then from there, I found there was a link to Whatever, the mailing list. And then that was it." When she says that was it, she means she found a community of fans, made lifelong friends, and eventually met her husband.

The mailing list was run by Ned Raggett, a grad student at the University of California, Irvine, who had unwittingly found himself in charge of a group of very, very eager fans. "Poor Ned," Sarah says, laughing. "He was like the principal of a very unruly school, just trying to keep order, and bless that man." Ned was a longtime music fan, and even in those very early days of the internet he was signed up for an internet mailing list for the band Sparks. When folks on campus in early 1995 wanted to test servers and other folks at the radio said they would help, they came up with the idea of seeing what it was like to run their own internet mailing lists for bands. "And we basically said, 'How many can we have?' And they said, 'Yeah, go for broke,'"

Ned recalls. "I think my friend Brian ended up running, like, ten lists, and I did it for a time, too," he says. "Being a Britpop listener in the mid-nineties, I basically cast the net wide and created lists for not just Oasis, but for a number of other bands, Suede, Pulp, the Boo Radleys, et cetera. I don't remember the exact time or date, but it was definitely '95, and it surely had to have been about the time that *What's the Story* was coming out. I put up the list, got it going, and I guess it was just the right time, because everything exploded."

The word of the new Oasis mailing list spread across the internet as it existed at the time—Usenet news groups, emails, and websites. "Those were your three options," explains Ned. Folks would sign up by emailing the majordomo email address and, once subscribed, could send messages to the Whatever email. Those emails would then go to everyone else on the mailing list. "When you subscribe, you have the option of either getting every message sent back individually, or subscribing in digest form, which would usually be about every twenty messages, not daily, every twenty messages," Ned notes. The mailing list really took off when Ned connected with a woman named Sarah (he can't remember her last name), who went by the user name Ginger. She was an American in San Diego who somehow had become the webmaster for Oasis's official website. "It was the unfortunately named Oasisinet.com, because someone already had Oasis.com and you had to do the work-around somehow," Ned says. It's still the address for the band's official website. Sarah put the information about the list on the band's official web page with the full instructions about how to join. "That absolutely blew things through the roof," Ned remembers. It was on the official web page that Sarah Connolly first learned about the list and joined the ensuing chaos.

The band was blowing up at this time not only on the music sales charts but in the press, too. They had graduated from being mainstays of the music news outlets and were now firmly tabloid fodder, and every bit of that gossip, tour news, rumors, song discussions, and more made its way to the mailing list. "This was the quickest way a lot of people could find out what the hell was going on with the band. But people could write anything they wanted to and, well, you sense what the issue can be, if anybody can write anything—and they can—you can theoretically get a lot of stuff. A lot of stuff. A lot of questions being asked over and over again," says Ned. "Sarah/Ginger, who was on the list, did participate and would say, like, 'No, guys, this is not true,' and helped very much keep on top of that." The fans swapped stories, news, and, especially for American fans who didn't have easy access to B-sides and the like, updates about releases and promos. "There was a definite hunger for as much information about the band, early demos, notable slash notorious live performances, things like that," says Ned.

Users came from around the world: the U.K., America, Canada, Europe, Japan, Hong Kong, Australia, New Zealand—the Anglosphere in general. "There were also very passionate fans from Central and South America, some very active Mexican fans," recalls Ned. "I remember a number of people from Brazil, Argentina." The result of this global fandom was that the mailing list was simply nonstop. "It was just a fire hose," Ned says, and it was extremely hard to manage. He still found a lot to love about the group. "There were relationships that happened through the list for a couple of years," he says. "I know at least three marriages resulted directly from the list . . . Lots of people made connections, sharing other music, helping each other, social aspects; people who knew each other could have meet-ups."

Still, it was a lot, because while Ned was an Oasis fan—he had gone to their early show at the Whisky a Go Go in L.A.—he wasn't a superfan by any means. He was also a grad student at the time, with a grad student's course load, and the list was slowly taking over his life. "Had I known beforehand it was going to be so chaotic, I don't quite know what I would have done. I like to think I would have still gone for it, but no regrets," he says now.

Luckily for Ned, at some point the internet expanded beyond mailing lists, and message boards became a thing. Sarah and many of her friends moved over to one called Oasis Fanatic, which is where she eventually met her husband, John. He's a Welsh man who she some-how convinced to move to Shreveport. "I met my husband on the Oasis message board, which is hysterical," she says. "Now we have two kids together, who would not exist were it not for that little band from Burnage and, god, I'm gonna cry. There was just something about them. This little band from Burnage who did not give a shit about what anybody else thought of them, and they were going to be loud and brash and do what they wanted. And, damn it, there's something freeing about that, you know?"

# MAPLE LEAF GARDENS,
## Toronto,
## January 15, 1998

Lisa Mark was twelve years old in the summer of 1996 and Canada's MuchMusic had *(What's the Story) Morning Glory?* in heavy rotation. "'Don't Look Back in Anger,' 'Champagne Supernova,' 'Wonderwall,' all those singles that came out during that time were on repeat," Lisa remembers. "It was either 'Don't Look Back in Anger' or 'Champagne Supernova' that first really grabbed my attention. It grabbed my heart. And then it was over—this was my favorite band forever."

She went and got the albums at her local HMV and begged for the box sets for Christmas. "And then it was the B-sides," she remembers. "Because I'd never even heard of a B-side, right? I didn't know what that was." She founded an Oasis fan club on the internet back in 1996 or 1997. "I called it the Liam Lovers Club, because, I was, like, twelve or thirteen," she says. "I got to meet so many fans from the U.K. and especially in Canada and the United States. It was great, because I didn't have any friends that liked Oasis, everybody hated them, everybody made fun of me and teased me because I loved them so much, and I just didn't care."

She wasn't able to see them live, though, until January 1998, when the *Be Here Now* tour set up at the Maple Leaf Gardens, an indoor hockey arena turned venue. "My mom called my school, and said, 'Hi, Lisa is not going to be in school today. She's got an appointment in Toronto,'" Lisa recalls. "She took me to my appointment in Toronto, which was seeing Noel Gallagher at MuchMusic. It was just the most exciting moment of my little life. I remember it was so freezing. I was so mad because we got there super early in the freezing, freezing cold, and we were all lined up outside the window at MuchMusic, and then they moved us all around, and they let in a few people, and I got screwed out of being on the inside. I was mad! We had been outside for about three hours in the absolute freezing cold, and I just remember everybody was singing because we were so cold, and we just wanted to see Noel so badly, even through the fogged glass. We were singing 'Don't Go Away' because of the line about the cold and frosty morning. If you watch the broadcast, you can see me in the window, and we were just pounding on the window because we were so excited to see him. He played 'Stand by Me.'"

Freezing outside the MuchMusic studio wasn't Lisa's only "appointment" in Toronto that day, though. She was going to see the band play that night, too. "I was super excited to see the gig because Noel had a solo set—he used to do these acoustic sets halfway through each Oasis show—and that actually didn't go on past the *Be Here Now* tour. So seeing a Noel acoustic set was a big deal. Also, other than Tony McCarroll, I got to see the original lineup of Oasis with Alan and Bonehead and Guigsy, and that was really cool for me. I remember I was so far away. We were way up in the stands. But I remember crying. I just cried and felt all the feels." Lisa was hooked and, luckily, so was her mom.

"She was a supportive parent, but she was a fan, too," says Lisa. "We drove down to Detroit and got a scalped ticket. It was an obstructed view, but it was side stage, and it turns out that you could see everything happening from the side, and all the bands would come out and watch the other bands. I had made a huge, huge, huge banner that had the Oasis logo in the Union Jack, so when Liam Gallagher came out to watch Blink-182 play—it was a radio Christmas show—he came and signed it. I got a photo talking to him, and I was wearing a Union Jack dress and everything."

The real highlight, though, was when she kinda sorta snuck backstage during their final tour through Canada in 2008. "I dropped a name that I happened to know from somebody who had to do with

the crew," she explains. "I'm not even kidding. I literally just walked up to this security guy, I dropped the name, and said, 'Oh, is this person around?' That's all I said, and the dude whips out a backstage pass and hands it to me. I was with my husband—he wasn't my husband yet—but the guy—he was British—looks at my husband and goes, 'He's got two chances to get back there: slim and fuck all.' So poor Justin had to go sit out in the car while I went backstage at the Oasis show and got to meet everybody. And Liam, in particular, was so wonderful that night. We couldn't find [bass player] Andy Bell anywhere in the meet-and-greet area, and Liam actually took me and paraded me all around through backstage just to find Andy Bell, just so he could sign my set list. He interrupted a private conversation he was having with some woman, and I felt so bad. I was so embarrassed, but when Liam Gallagher is doing that, you just let him do it." She adds, "It was just the highlight of my life."

She also had a memorable moment with Noel when she mentioned reading the travelogue he had been sharing on the web. "Noel was so funny that night because he had been writing a blog. He called it *Tales from the Middle of Nowhere*, but it was basically a series of stories, and I remember I said, 'I've been following your blog,' and his eyes just about hit the ceiling. It was so funny. And he goes, 'Blog?' And I'm like, 'Yeah, you know, your blog that you're writing, or whatever.' And it was so funny, the very next entry into the blog was: 'This is not a blog. Someone mentioned the B-word yesterday. Blogs are for people with no friends.' It's so funny."

The photo with Liam, the signed set list, and the signed Union Jack poster kick-started a love of collecting for Lisa, who has a Union Jack guitar signed by Noel, a tambourine that Liam threw her, a Gem

Archer set list, and a Vox Box, a very rare U.K. promotional item that looks like a mini amp filled with CDs. "It is like the holy grail for Oasis fans," she says. "Noel Gallagher signed that in New York years ago." However, the best souvenir she picked up at an Oasis show was probably her husband, Justin. "What year, honey?" "2005," Justin supplies from the background. Their wedding rings have Oasis tributes in them, of course. "I wrote, 'And we can slide away' from 'Slide Away' inside Justin's, and he wrote, 'I heart you Oasis girl,' because that was my license plate for my car: O-A-S-I-S-G-I-R-L."

They pay homage to the band that brought them together in other ways, too. "It'll be twenty years since we met when we see them at the reunion, and we're taking our kids, Liam and Jill," she says. Lest you think Lisa and Justin missed the opportunity to name their daughter Lyla or Sally, like real fans, Jill is actually a deep cut of a reference. She is named after longtime Oasis photographer Jill Furmanovsky, who helped inspire Lisa to become a rock photographer herself.

# UNIVERSAL AMPHITHEATER,
## Los Angeles,
## January 27–28, 1998

Tina Snell was soaking wet. She was barely out of the shower, wrapped in a towel, and her hair was dripping, but she needed to turn up the song on the radio. "I had never heard anything like it," she says. It was, of course, Oasis.

She was a kid in San Diego, listening to 91X FM, and she liked what they were playing. Growing up, Tina's family listened to a lot of music, but none of it was *hers* per se. "My family had kind of eclectic tastes. My mom is white, my dad's Black, so there's a lot of pop, rap and hip-hop, and R&B in our house growing up," she says. "I don't think that, prior to Oasis, I'd really had a band that I loved. Music that I could say, 'Oh, this is for me.' It kind of flipped the switch inside.

"I actually borrowed the *Morning Glory* CD from a friend because I couldn't go buy one. I didn't have any money," she recalls. She eventually bought her own copy, and then *Definitely Maybe*, and then started to dive into the import singles. "My dad had given me some money as a gift, and I took some of it and immediately drove to Tower Records to buy the 'Wonderwall' U.K. single because it had an additional song on it that the U.S. version didn't have," she says. She was hooked. "By the time the third album came out, those were the only three discs in my giant three-disc CD changer," she remembers. "I would play Oasis on the way to dropping my brother off at school. I would also play Oasis to my little sister, who was, like, two years old at the time, and my parents would roll their eyes. We had a cute, full-circle moment recently. Noel Gallagher did a solo tour, and I took my brother and my sister to the concert."

She wouldn't exactly call her family fans of the band, but she still had to bring her mom and her little sister with her to her first Oasis show. "It was during the *Be Here Now* tour at the Universal Amphitheater in L.A. I wasn't allowed to go to concerts until I was eighteen, and I still lived at home in college, and my mom and dad were like, 'You're not going up to L.A. for a concert by yourself.' So I went and got a hotel room at the hotel that was closest to the venue, because I was like, 'Oh, I want to see the band members and I'm sure they'll be in the hotel next door,'" she says, laughing at her naiveté. "I went to the concert, and my mom and my sister stayed in the hotel room until I got back. It was a wonderful experience. Even just trying to buy the tickets, I was such a newbie to the entire process. I didn't understand that there were pit tickets, so when I bought my concert ticket at Tower Records, they were like, 'Well, where do you want to sit?' And I said the very first row, the very first seat. I wanted to be as close as I could be. And then I got there that night to discover, 'Oh, there's, like, six rows of people in front of me.' I just didn't know there was such a thing as a pit! I didn't have that experience."

Still, she made the most of her night. She brought a camera and took as many photos as she could and picked up more than a few souvenirs. "I was so incredibly excited to see Oasis that I bought every single shirt that they had on sale. I think I bought everything that they had," she says. "There was a jacket pinned up and I bought the one off the wall. I chatted up the security guard telling him, 'I need a souvenir from this show,' and he gave me his little, like, call sheet for the night and some earplugs."

She went and saw Oasis ten more times and, after the band broke up, she saw the brothers' solo performances somewhere in the double digits. "Have shows, will travel," she states. "I try to see as many as I can, because it has been proven these are some fickle people, and it's not like they need the money, so you never know when they're gonna pack it in. I think Noel's last [solo] tour, I saw, like, eight or ten of the dates. I have had people ask me, 'Why would you go see the same show over and over?' Because if you had the opportunity to have the best night of your life more than once, why would you not do that?"

# PART III

# 2000-2009

After writing three albums, largely on his own, for the band's fourth release, Noel started sharing the songwriting responsibilities with his other bandmates, including Liam. The result was *Standing on the Shoulder of Giants*, which dabbled in psychedelia, electronica, and synthesizer rock and gave fans something to think about. The album recording process had been difficult, because Paul "Bonehead" Arthurs had quit in the middle of it, followed a few weeks later by Paul "Guigsy" McGuigan, the bass guitar player. Their parts were rerecorded for the album. Before the tour, guitarist Gem Archer and bass player Andy Bell, a legend in his own right, thanks to his time in the Welsh outfit, Ride, joined the band.

Oasis had been touring for most of the year 2000 to promote the not especially well-received album. While critics were not impressed, fans, particularly young fans who may not have been able to see the band's earlier shows, were still more than happy to buy enough tickets to sell out stadiums around the world. Such was the case when Steven Morris came to Reebok Stadium in Bolton that July.

"It was my first kind of big concert, so it was amazing," he recalls. "We wanted to make the most of it, so we ended up pestering my friend's mum, who was taking us, to make sure that we got there as early as possible. We saw every single support act, even the ones who we didn't think were very good. We just wanted to experience that whole day. I think we were in the stadium from about three o'clock onwards, and I think Oasis came on just after nine p.m., so yeah, I think her mum was thoroughly fed up by the end. The things people do for their children. So, *Standing on the Shoulder of Giants* wasn't my favorite album, if I'm honest, but obviously it was still amazing to be part of it, and obviously they played all of the big hits. So yeah, that was the first time I saw them."

The thing is, though, Steven didn't actually *see* them. That's because he was born fully blind, and through a hereditary condition had slowly lost most of his hearing, too, although he still retains some. He also loves music and loves going to concerts, a fact that stumps some people. He explains, "Most people who would be classified as deaf-blind aren't totally deaf and totally blind. It's very much a spectrum. There will be people who are completely deaf and completely blind. There'll be people like me who've got no sight, but some hearing. There'll be people who've got some sight and some hearing."

Like many other Oasis devotees, Steven heard Oasis on the radio and quickly became a fan. "It was in 1995 when 'Wonderwall' was released. I was eleven years old, and then I heard that song on the radio, and I was like, 'Oh my gosh, this is amazing,'" he says. That Christmas he got both *Definitely Maybe* and *What's the Story* and started listening to the cassettes on repeat.

"I listened to them in my room at home. I listened to them in my Walkman when I was out. I went to boarding school, so I listened to them all the time there as well," he says. "I eventually got them on CD because the cassettes probably got worn out quite quickly."

For him the band and their music were the perfect escape. "They were the first band or artist that I became, like, properly obsessed with," he says. "I wanted all of their music, including the bootlegs and the stuff you shouldn't have, like random demo versions that were never meant to see the light of day. I just wanted all of it. I wanted to talk about them all the time," he remembers. "And when I was growing up, I didn't have that many friends, so I kind of escaped really into books and music and Oasis were my big thing at the time."

Like many other boys his age, Steven wanted to be Liam or Noel Gallagher when he grew up. "Sadly, I didn't have the talent to be either," he says. "I was a drummer, though, so the closest I was ever going to become to being Oasis was to be the next Tony McCarroll or Alan White. That was the limit of my aspirations in the end." Unlike other boys his age, Steven didn't really know what the Gallaghers looked like or dressed like. "The only thing that I really had to go on in terms of what they looked like, back when I was a child, was when one of the older members of my family disapprovingly said how scruffy Liam looked in his big parka," he says, laughing. "If I had known what they looked like, I would probably have been pestering my mum for a Liam-esque parka." He notes that these days there's technology that will describe photos, so now he has a bit more of an idea of what they look like.

Steven saw the band one more time, during the *Dig Out Your Soul* tour, the band's last hurrah before breaking up in Paris. "I saw them one more time in 2009, just before they split up, in Cardiff in Wales," he recalls. "That was in June 2009, and I think they split up in August. So I saw them in the middle of their prime, and then at the end of their careers."

If you're curious what it's like to go to a concert as someone with visual impairment, Steven says it's still very much a good time. "You just listen, and you can kind of vibe off them, and you can hear it, obviously," he says. "Yeah, you can hear like all of the noise around you. I haven't been to a gig as big as seeing Oasis in Cardiff until I saw Taylor Swift in Cardiff last year—and you could definitely hear that crowd. That was next-level kind of noise. In Cardiff, which was like seventy or eighty thousand, people who can see say it's an amazing sight to just see all of those people, but you know you can certainly hear them even when you're hearing-impaired."

It's not just the noise, though, he says: "I think it's really just about being part of that crowd and experiencing the noise and the excitement, and obviously people like pushing forward to be at the front. Certainly when we saw them in Cardiff, we were right at the front where the barriers were. To be honest, I could probably have done with being a bit further back. But I certainly knew when Oasis were coming onstage because everybody threw their beer. And sadly, being at the front meant that I got my hair full. I mean, I certainly hope it was beer. I *trust* that it was beer." It is clear that Steven knows it most likely was not beer.

Despite all the, um, beer, Steven did hope to see the band's reunion tour. However, he was unable to secure a ticket. "I'm pretty gutted about it," he admits, but he hasn't given up hope of being able to experience it a little bit from home. "I'm hoping that at least, if I can't experience it in person, I can experience it on somebody's dodgy stream."

# WEMBLEY STADIUM,
## London,
## July 21–22, 2000

After playing the smaller Wembley Arena, Oasis had finally graduated to Wembley Stadium. However, what was supposed to be a highlight of the *Standing on the Shoulder of Giants* tour turned into a nightmare.

The band's performance at Wembley was widely regarded as a disaster and seen by many as their worst-ever live show. Liam reportedly arrived onstage drunk, talking trash to the crowd, and forgetting or failing to sing the words to many of their most beloved songs. That was particularly unfortunate, as the second night of the show was set to be broadcast on television and to be recorded for a live album.

Band tensions were already running high, as Noel had taken a hiatus from the group in May after a fight with his brother, where Liam allegedly questioned the paternity of Noel's daughter. Noel skipped the rest of the international tour, returning for the U.K. dates, including the Wembley gig. *NME* reported that during the second Wembley show, Liam and Noel were so tense that it "frequently seemed set to come to blows." In 2017, Noel told Radio X: "[That was] the low point in Oasis. It was a horrible two and a half hours onstage. Liam can hang his head in shame. It was dreadful." Liam has since said, also in a Radio X interview, that he has not drunk booze onstage since that infamous concert.

While the shows, particularly the second night, are considered to be some of the band's worst performances, the fans didn't necessarily care. At least the fans who snuck out to Wembley to see the show without ever telling their parents.

Jenny Stevens was around nine years old when she first heard "Supersonic," or maybe "Live Forever," on the dusty radio in her dad's builder's van. Like many other fans, she just fell for it. She watched *Top of the Pops* religiously and recorded *The Chart Show* onto her boom box every week, always looking for the next big sound, and for her it was Oasis. "I was completely hooked from when I first heard it. I thought Liam's voice was incredible. I was just completely gripped by the swagger," she recalls.

Now the deputy features editor at *The Guardian*, Jenny associates Oasis, particularly the second album, with a tough time in her family's life. "My family were made homeless when I was about ten," she says. "We lived in a homeless hostel for a while. It was bleak. My dad was a builder and always out of work, because there just isn't any work when the economy tanks. It was really difficult. Then we were rehoused on an estate called Whitehawk in Brighton, which was one of two estates where no one would ever go. It was a sink estate, essentially, which was a kind of new term at that point for the way certain areas in England, well, probably in the U.K., had been ring-fenced off and just dumped, essentially. They had terrible schools, terrible transport links, everyone was out of work. I remember it being really bleak. There were piles of rubbish everywhere. There was dog shit everywhere. It was a mess. All these sorts of things that happened in the nineties, like teen pregnancies and glue-sniffing, lots of open drug use, joyriding, all of this stuff was going on outside the window. But I remember music being played constantly. When *(What's the Story) Morning Glory?* came out, and the opening of that album, and the guitars and the sort of volume of it, I remember it was just played *everywhere*. I remember that music and that sound just ringing through the whole estate, all the time. That album was just constantly on."

The music of Oasis was omnipresent at a time when Jenny was getting older and recognizing more about the world around her. "It gave me a sense of connection and belonging in a way," she says. "We moved onto that estate when I was about eleven, so I was really coming to terms with what class was. What my parents didn't have, compared to what my friends had; that my dad was always in the dole queue and that wasn't his fault, there just wasn't work. It was just this sort of entrenched feeling of being ignored and left behind, and there just not really being anything to work for or get a job for, which is kind of what 'Cigarettes & Alcohol' is all about, you know? What is the point of it all? Because nothing works and everything's broken, and we're poor and it's shit. And I just sort of felt this sense of connection with the lyrics and with the music. I wasn't a twenty-year-old stoner in a parka from Manchester. I was essentially a little girl in Brighton, but I definitely felt it all around me, and I felt it in my family, and I could see it out the windows. I found that really powerful. And I do think it was an early political awakening. It was like, 'Oh, other people feel like this, too,' and there's kind of a power in that."

When *Be Here Now* was released in 1997, Jenny stood in line all night outside a shop in Brighton to be among the first to hear the new album. And when Oasis came to Wembley Stadium in 2000, Jenny and her best friend did what many independent-minded fifteen-year-old kids did: said they were sleeping at each other's houses and jumped onto a coach to London. Jenny wrote about this in *The Guardian* in 2024, which is how her friend's mom finally found out about their subterfuge. Jenny had a job in a bakery and saved up some money to buy a ticket, and she and her friend hopped onto a bus in Brighton with "a twenty-pound note and nothing else" and rode to Wembley. "We were dramatically younger than everyone else on the coach," she recalls, laughing. "Now I'm just like, 'God, that was wild.' Like, there were grown men smoking crack on the bus. It was very chaotic. We got there quite early because we wanted to see the support bands, and Doves were playing, and Black Grape. It was such an event. They broadcast it live on the TV. It felt like this huge, exciting moment."

The gig was pretty much everything she had dreamed of. "I have overwhelmingly fond memories of that day," she says. "It's quite rare where you go to a gig where it very much feels like you've just waited to be there for so long, and it means so much to you because you're so young."

While she was young and forgiving, it wasn't all fun, though. "What I really remember is just so many men and so many very rowdy, raucous men. I remember getting grabbed on the bum, and that was the first time I got groped at a gig, and it was shit. There was a lot of jumping about, a lot of men weeing in beer glasses and throwing it. I mean, I don't think the crowd was particularly savory by then," she says. "I guess that was sort of the cusp of where people just got tired of going to those gigs. And I have to say, I didn't really want to, either, by the time I was an older teenager. I could have gone to see a lot more Oasis shows, but I just didn't. You knew what the crowds were going to be like and it just wasn't really where I wanted to be. I mean, by that point, I had an asymmetric haircut, and was really into electroclash, so probably wasn't going to be hanging out at Oasis gigs, but there was definitely this feeling that it wasn't really the place for a young woman anymore, which is sad."

Still, she loved being at Wembley. "I could barely hear anything, I could barely see anything, but I was having the absolute time of my life, and getting covered in beer and piss, but I kind of didn't care," she says. "It was totally joyous."

# SHEPHERD'S BUSH EMPIRE,
## London,
## October 7–8, 2001

After months of globe-trotting that took them across England to Thailand, Venezuela, and New York's Radio City Music Hall in support of their fourth album, *Standing on the Shoulder of Giants*, Oasis had one more tour in them that year. To mark their tenth anniversary, the band scheduled six dates across the U.K., where they played in smaller venues and put together a set list of all their hits from the last decade. The 10 Years of Noise & Confusion Tour kicked off with two nights at Shepherd's Bush in London. Patrick Schmidt had flown to London from Philadelphia with the hope that the paper ticket he bought off eBay would actually get him in the door.

Patrick first heard Oasis on the local radio show *Planet M*, hosted by Matt Cord on the Philadelphia radio station WMMR. That wasn't what hooked him, though. "I ended up going to four different colleges, and I hated every second of college. And I was at RIT, which is in Rochester, New York, and it was, snowing in October, and I was like, 'What am I doing here?'" he remembers. "I went to the record store and I bought a single that had 'Acquiesce' on it. I put it on in my car, and the second song came on, I knew. I got back to my dorm room and called my friend Steve, and I was like, 'Holy shit, you have to go to the record store right now and buy this.' I played it for him over the phone, like, held up the rotary phone to the stereo and played it for him."

He went to see them as often as he could after that. "I saw them at the TLA [Theatre of Living Arts] on South Street in Philadelphia on the second leg of the *Definitely Maybe* tour, which fits maybe four or five hundred, and then they came back in '96 at the Tower Theater for *What's the Story.* And from that time on, I went to every show that was either in New York, Boston, or Philadelphia. I worked in alternative radio, so I was able to use that when I needed to, but I would always buy the tickets. I didn't care." He flew to see them in Reading in 1999 and Glastonbury in 2004, and when he heard about their ten-year anniversary show, he wanted to go, but needed to figure out the ticket situation.

"For the 10 Years of Noise and Confusion Tour, I bought a ticket off of eBay, and I was like, 'This is going to be a fake ticket,'" he says, laughing. "I always tried to go see Oasis as much as I could, and seeing them in the U.K. at that point was obviously a very different experience than seeing them here in the U.S. It was the tenth anniversary of the band and they were doing an underplay." For those who don't work in the music industry like Patrick, an underplay is when a wildly popular band plays at a tiny venue, playing for under the number of tickets they could sell. Like when Nirvana with Joan Jett and Kim Gordon played the diminutive Saint Vitus in Brooklyn, when they could have sold out Madison Square Garden. "Shepherd's Bush Empire is probably a two-thousand-person venue, and they could sell eighty thousand tickets in the U.K., no problem," he explains. "But I really wanted to go." Patrick had used eBay since the early days of the online auction house, which was founded in 1995. At some point concert tickets started popping up on the site, serving as a makeshift secondary marketplace in the days before StubHub and Ticketmaster started reselling. "I saw a ticket for sale for the tour, but it was like two hundred or four hundred dollars, I can't remember which, but at that time, for me, it was a lot of money," he says. "I emailed the seller, and he said that he had won it on the lottery, and they mailed it to him in the mail, which would have been accurate. He was in Virginia, though, which was weird. He said he wanted to go, but couldn't. And he showed me a picture of the ticket, because it had custom artwork on it, like all the U.K. tickets did. And I was just like, 'Okay,' and I bought it. I won the auction and then it came in the mail, and I was looking at it, and I was just like, 'I guess this is real.' And I flew out. I landed that morning. The show was that night. I was convinced that when I would get there that the ticket would be counterfeit and I wouldn't be able to go to the show, but it wasn't. They let me in and I had way too much fun. And then I came home. I still have the ticket. It's actually a pretty cool ticket, because it says '10 Years of Noise and Confusion,' and that's the only Oasis T-shirt I own, too. I bought it there, because the merch was so bad forever, like, embarrassingly bad. But yeah, in hindsight, buying a ticket off eBay maybe was pretty silly."

Patrick returned to buying tickets from unlikely sources on the internet, when it came to seeing the band at Wembley Stadium in July 2009. Patrick is good friends with Miguel Banuelos, who saw them play at Liberty Lunch in Texas in 1995, and they had flown over to see Oasis play two nights at Wembley Stadium in London. "The first night we sat in the seats, but Miguel had never seen Oasis in the U.K., and I really wanted him to be on the floor, the general-admission area, because that's the real experience," Patrick explains. "I went on Craigslist in the U.K., and I was just like, 'Hey, I'm looking to trade my VIP tickets for GA tickets.' I had VIP tickets for some bullshit VIP area in Wembley, and it was lame and no one was having fun in those seats, and I didn't care about it. So I posted on Craigslist looking to switch with someone for a GA ticket, and this college student emailed me. He was trying to take his girlfriend to the show, but she was scared to be on the floor. So I was like, 'Cool, let's meet.' We met in the walkway from the subway to the stadium and he showed up and we switched. That was very memorable, because Miguel got to be on the floor, and it was actually a good show, too. But that's also when they started with throwing the piss, which is fucking disgusting, but we had a great time."

The first and last time Andrew Schiffman saw Oasis was at the Coachella Valley Music and Arts Festival in Indio, California, in 2002. The problem is, he doesn't really remember it. "I was there," he says. "I have the ticket stub to prove I was there, but I was so drunk I don't remember anything, exactly."

It was only the third time the festival had been put on and Oasis were headlining along with their former Knebworth support acts, the Prodigy and the Chemical Brothers. Also headlining the festival were Björk, the Foo Fighters, and Pete Yorn. While Coachella is Coachella, the show was ostensibly a part of the tour in support of their 2002 album, *Heathen Chemistry*. That was the first album recorded with new members Gem Archer and Andy Bell, who contributed to the songwriting, and the last to feature drummer Alan White. The tour would eventually be marked by several major incidents including a car accident that put Noel, bassist Andy Bell, and touring keyboardist Jay Darlington in the hospital and a bar brawl in Munich that cost time, money, and, in Liam's case, some teeth. But that day in the California desert it was just sun, songs, and a crowd of fans who were mad for it. "I know we were just dancing and having a good time," remembers Andrew. "Every song's an anthem, so you're just screaming the words with everyone."

Andrew was born an Oasis fan. "Growing up in London, being an Oasis fan, it's just in your blood. It's in your culture," he says. "Oasis are like the royal family." Andrew had a bunch of friends fly in from London for Coachella, and through Andrew's connections in the music world, they had scored VIP tickets. "It was an amazing show, but if I would have known that was the last time I was going to see them, I would have probably appreciated it a lot more."

Luckily Andrew was able to show his appreciation for the band in other ways. The U.S. market had always been slightly difficult for Oasis to crack. Not that Noel cared, as *The Guardian* reports he once said, "I don't give a fuck about America as long as they buy the fucking records." Still, Andrew wanted to do his part to boost the band, and he was in a position to do it. He was working at MTV programming and helped bring back the channel's iconic *120 Minutes* program with its focus on alternative rock. "Oasis wasn't supported too much in the U.S. market with radio, but at MTV and MTV2, I really did have an opportunity to take advantage of my position and play their videos more," he says. "I would come up with, like, 'Across the Pond' playlists, and would feature a couple of their videos in there. I used my power to support them as much as someone in my position programming videos for MTV2 could."

He was working at MTV in 2009 when he heard the news that Oasis broke up. "You just don't think it's real and you don't believe it's forever," he says. "You know, you hear bands breaking up and then coming back. I was very deep having my ear to the ground for years, hearing rumblings of 'Yes, they're going to get back together. They have to wait till Noel's kids are eighteen, then he won't have to give child support to his wife.' So we almost had this time frame in our minds because of things I had heard internally. And I guess it was true."

Andrew got tickets to see them in New York City, where he lives, as well as in his hometown of London. "I paid full price," he says. "It's one of the first—one of the only—concerts I've really paid for." That is definitely the sign of a true fan.

# TWEETER CENTER,
## Mansfield, Massachusetts,
## June 24, 2005

The sixth studio album by Oasis, *Don't Believe the Truth*, was supposed to come out in the summer or fall of 2004, but they struggled to find a sound and a set of songs that made the band and the label happy. They had initially returned to Sawmills Studios, where they recorded the first album, but things weren't working. They then went to Wheeler End Studios, where Noel and Dave Sardy served as the producers, with the other members once again contributing to the songwriting. The band, now with Zak Starkey behind the drum kit, eventually came up with a track listing that made everyone happy, and the album was released in May 2005 with "Lyla" as the first single. Once again the band got ready to hit the road for a long worldwide tour that would take them to twenty-six countries and have over 3.2 million fans singing along to their songs, including Brian Garcia, who had been waiting for years for a chance to see them play.

"MTV used to run small commercials called MTV Buzz Clips, and they would run, like, a thirty-second montage of the hottest music of the time," Brian remembers. He recalls one summer in the months after Kurt Cobain died watching MTV and seeing a montage that included the Stone Temple Pilots and Portishead before cutting to some kid singing about living forever. "I still remember sitting on my grandmother's living room floor and watching the TV and seeing that play and remembering how it affected me," he says. "I was like, 'Whoa.' It made me pause. The world disappeared around me. It captured me in a way that no other line had. I'm totally serious about that. What a massive line, and I liked the music. But I didn't know who it was, because MTV didn't say who it was. They were just playing clips and went on to the next commercial."

Brian headed to CD Warehouse, the main record store in his small Texas town, and shyly sang the line from the song to the guy working there and asked him if he knew who it might be. "He snaps his fingers and goes, 'Oh yeah, that's a new band out of England, they're called Oasis,'" Brian recalls. He went over to the wall of CDs and grabbed *Definitely Maybe*. It was a decision that would eventually cost him well over $1 million.

Brian took the *Definitely Maybe* CD home, and in case this story wasn't nineties enough for you, he put it into the CD-ROM player in his computer and listened while he hung out in some chat rooms. He liked what he heard, but he wasn't quite in love yet. That would happen a few months later, when MTV played "Don't Look Back in Anger" for the first time.

Brian was delivering tortillas for his grandparents' business, but when he heard that MTV was premiering a new song from Oasis, he snuck out of work to watch it. "I went to my uncle's house because it was right next door, and he had a big-screen TV—one of those huge box big-screen TVs—and I was sitting on his blue fabric recliner, and I just remember turning on the big screen, and just from the opening chord, and just the visual of English culture, the look, the style, the sound, I fell into, like, this ocean of love," he says. "It just pervaded like every single part of my body. It went into every fingertip, every tip of my toes, like the top of my head, that you just felt it all over my body. It sounds silly, but that was truly like one of the more special moments in my life." Brian found himself fully in the deep end of an Oasis obsession. However, living in a small town in West Texas, he didn't have many opportunities or the money to see them. He finally made a plan in 2005 for the *Don't Believe the Truth* tour.

"My girlfriend at the time, we drove from Texas to Boston to watch Oasis," he says. "In 2005 I was going to the University of Texas, and I had the means. I had my own car. So my girlfriend and I went to Boston. We made a road trip around the U.S. out of it, and I made some really great friends there that are still like my best friends today."

Brian and his girlfriend rolled into the parking lot of the Tweeter Center in Mansfield, a suburb of Boston, about five hours early for the concert. "We painted my car with Oasis stuff all over it. It was a black Escalade. It had 'Oasis' painted on the back and had a Union Jack. It was really pretty. They thought I was part of the band," he says, laughing. "We hung out in the front. We played songs outside. It was the most special moment because of the friends, and it was the first time, and there were new feelings. It was a spectacle. It is one thing to witness a party, but another thing is to be in the middle, and the one celebrating it. It's just much different."

Brian is a collector at heart, so it was only a matter of time until he started amassing Oasis memorabilia. The first item in his collection was a promo coin to commemorate *Standing on the Shoulder of Giants.* They reportedly made only two hundred of them and Brian got one. "Oasis had only been around for, like, six years, and they were at their height when I was starting my collection," he explains. "So I was just getting whatever was available commercially. When you're the biggest band in the world, you're not going to be selling your guitars and amps." He picked up promo items, coins, a cigarette lighter, T-shirts, a Vox Box. As he gathered more items, people started to reach out to him, offering bigger and better items, like crew member jackets, awards, gold discs, demo and master tapes, guitars, lyrics, and more and more. He even has drummer Tony McCarroll's passport from when he was touring with Oasis. He has items that Noel Gallagher himself was shocked to see again, like a gold disc for *(What's the Story) Morning Glory?* that had been presented to Paul Weller. "I've got all of Andy's basses. I've got two of Guigsy's basses. I've got Gem's guitar. I have Noel's guitars. I have Liam's coat that he wore at the BRIT Awards. I have Bonehead's 'Champagne Supernova' jacket. The hat from the 'Wonderwall' music video. I have the 'Wonderwall' middle finger *NME* award. It just goes on and on," Brian says. The collection is around 3,500 to 4,000 pieces, if you include CDs and set lists and smaller items, Brian estimates.

"If I had to give it all up, except for one item, it would be Tony's drum kit. The one that was played at the Boardwalk, the one that was used to record all of *Definitely Maybe*, and it was used to record their first number one single, 'Some Might Say,'" Brian says.

While Brian loves his collection and collecting, he is at his heart a superfan of the band. He has traveled extensively to see them, spent time and money to build his collection, and even named his daughters Oasis Jolie and Nirvana Supernova. Still, the most important thing Oasis brought him—and why he loves the band so much—is the community he found among the fans.

"Being an Oasis fan is about being taken in and being accepted and being loved. The fans really made that, and I think that's the one special thing about Oasis," he says. "And I'll tell you something right now, as we're interviewing, inside of my restaurant, right now is a guy who came from Georgia to come see my collection. He brought his whole family. He just pulled in about twenty, thirty minutes ago. He came specifically to see my collection from Georgia with his family, and we're about to go to my house so I can show it to him. I'm not even going to ask any questions. He's an Oasis fan, and with fans it's just unspoken that you're just automatically going to love everybody.

"I think that's why Oasis means so much," he says, "because Oasis is not only about the music, but about its community."

---

One of the lifelong friends that Brian made at that Oasis show outside Boston is Evan Grondski. Evan got to experience a little of the generous spirit of the Oasis fan community that day.

"I got there at about eleven a.m., even before security showed up, and saw [Brian]," he says. "He and I were the first people there, so we kind of shacked up next to each other and had a memorable time hanging out before the show as everyone was filtering in. It was a really great show, met a lot of cool people, met up with a lot of cool people. Probably the coolest memory, though, was someone who I was just kind of having a chat with in the parking lot called me over and said, 'Oh, a friend of mine couldn't come and I want you to have this ticket.' It was third row. It was a ticket I couldn't afford at the time. And I was like, 'Well, what do you want for it? I got sixty bucks.' And the guy said, 'No, I just want it to go to someone who will really appreciate it.' I don't remember this guy's name, I don't even really remember where he's from, but it was just a random, pay-it-forward-type interaction, and I was really grateful for that. You can see me in the video of that concert that's up on YouTube. Just me right there, right up front. It was amazing."

Evan grew up a Beatles fan and was intrigued by all the buzz surrounding Oasis that compared them to Liverpool's Fab Four. He picked up *What's the Story* in seventh grade or so, and enjoyed it, but didn't think much about the band until around 1998, when *The Masterplan*, a collection of B-sides and live tracks, came out in the United States. "I remember a woman on the radio saying that it included a cover of 'I Am the Walrus,' and being a Beatles fan it prompted me to take a look at it the next time I was in the record store," he says. So he rode his bike down to Words and Music in Fairhaven, Massachusetts, and picked up a copy of the compilation.

"I was really blown away by those songs. It just really surprised me that the songs were so good and they didn't make the record," he says. "So after kind of falling in love with some of those songs, it just put me on the journey of going back and listening to the other records, and I just became a fan of those songs and the band." He saw Oasis live for the first time in 2001 during the Tour of Brotherly Love, which featured Oasis, the Black Crowes, and Spacehog, three rock bands with three pairs of famously quarrelsome brothers. Evan was a junior in high school and his girlfriend's mom drove them up to the Tweeter Center in Mansfield, Massachusetts, for the show. It's safe to say that Evan had a good time. "I couldn't talk for a couple of days because I probably blew my voice out somewhere around the third song," he says, laughing. "'Columbia' was massive live. It was great to see them live. I had kind of been living my Oasis fandom over the internet at the time, through different message forums and whatnot, so it was kind of nice to live it out in real life, if you will." He saw Oasis many more times, including at Madison Square Garden, a show at New York's Jones Beach, and at the Narrows Festival on Staten

Island. He also started collecting a few odds and ends of memorabilia, too. "Not like Brian," he says, laughing.

What is like Brian, though, is that Evan thinks about the impact of Oasis on his life, not in terms of the music, but in terms of the friends he made along the way. "The big thing is, the band's brought me to so many interesting people in so many different areas of the world. It's just been a great connector to some really interesting, lifelong friendships," he says. "It's just cool to know that, basically, every time I travel for most tours, wherever I go, I'm going to know some people that are there, that I can hang out with, have a couple of drinks, catch up, and put the songs on the jukebox, and we all know every word."

———

Brian and Evan met one more person in the parking lot of that show at the Tweeter Center—Tina Snell, who first saw Oasis at the Universal Amphitheater back in 1998. She was living in Boston at the time and, naturally, went to go see Oasis play. "I know Evan and I know Brian because I've seen the same people at concerts for fifteen-plus years, maybe even twenty years now," she says. "I just remember them being in the parking lot and they were just doing some pregaming, and I was like, 'These kids are so *loud*.' I'm a little older than them. Then I saw them inside, and then I saw them again at another concert, and Evan and I connected somehow, and I don't even know how we got to be friends. I think it was mostly that we just kept seeing each other over and over."

These days, Tina plans on it. "I go not only to see the band and hear the music, but I go to see my friends that I've made through these experiences. These are people I send holiday cards to now. These are people who I have watched their kids grow up online. These are some of my longest friendships, and I got them from Oasis. I'm super eternally grateful for the music, but I'm even more grateful for the people that I met."

While she still usually buys merch at the shows, at each concert she goes to, Tina makes her ever-expanding group of friends little mementos. "I always end up putting together, like, bracelets or buttons or some kind of merch that I've facilitated to remember that we were all at the show together. And those are the things that I cherish."

Tina is a dedicated fan and is really good at connecting with other dedicated Oasis fans. "One of my really good friends, Bernadette [from the Whiskey a Go Go show], I met her and her friend Christie in line in San Diego at a Noel Gallagher solo show. We were waiting for Noel, because it's pretty well known that on his little tours he'll come out early and sign autographs. So I was waiting out there, and we were waiting forever. I got there super early, and there were a few other people there, and I was like, 'How do I not know you? Like, San Diego is my hometown. How many of us are going to be here this early for this one guy?' We were waiting a really long time, and I had a plastic container of candy in the back of my Jeep, and I was like, 'Well, does anyone want to snack?' And then I ordered a pizza, and I was handing out slices to people who wanted them, and that's how we met. And then it was very easy to trade Facebook info and Instagram info, and now these are friends. It's like when you're in third grade, 'Oh, I like cookies. Do you like cookies? Yay. Now we're best friends.' A lot of it has been like that. Like, 'Oh, do you want a [souvenir] button?' I make or order buttons and they come in, like, the hundreds, so after I've given them to my friends, I'll give them to the kids. It didn't cost me very much, but it's just a souvenir. That makes me feel good. And I've met a lot of people just by giving them something. I do think you get what you give. And if I can gain a friend by handing out a button, why not?"

# CITY OF MANCHESTER STADIUM,
## Manchester,
## June 30–July 3, 2005

Whenever Oasis played Manchester, it was a massive homecoming celebration. It was even more special when they were able to play on the home turf of the Gallaghers' beloved Man City football team. So when the *Don't Believe the Truth* tour stopped for a three-day residency at the City of Manchester Stadium it was a raucous three days in front of a riotous hometown crowd. A lineup of supporting bands including Super Furry Animals, the Coral, and fellow Mancunians Doves played to a packed house of nearly sixty thousand people. In their review of the opening-night show, *NME* noted that as the crowd roared their approval, "an emotional Noel Gallagher applaud[ed] the crowd" right back.

One of the fans Noel was applauding from the stage had been waiting nearly ten years to see his favorite band. James Lees grew up in a small village called Lazenby, outside Middlesbrough in the U.K., and like many kids in 1995 all he wanted for Christmas was a copy of *(What's the Story) Morning Glory?*, which he played on his very first CD player. "I picked up *(What's the Story) Morning Glory?* and I put the CD in, and as soon as you press play all you hear is the faintest sounds of 'Wonderwall,' very, very like quietly. So what do I do? I whack that CD up to play up to full volume. This is super great, and the next thing, this 'boing boing' comes in, and then the first track of the album, 'Hello,' just blasts out," he recalls. "I just said, 'Oh my god,' and next thing you know, Mum and Dad are shouting from downstairs, 'What's that noise?!' I loved it. They just became my band from then on."

However, despite the long-running love of the band, he didn't see them live until 2005. "Because of my background and where I grew up, there really was no chance of me going to see Oasis, and being able to afford a ticket was nonexistent as a young teenager. Growing up, Mum and Dad didn't have the money to take me there," James says. He finally got the chance during the *Don't Believe the Truth* tour.

"My friend's uncle had seen Oasis a couple of times previous, and he said, 'I know you and your mate, Lees'—me being Lees—'love Oasis, do you want me to get you tickets? If I get some, we can all drive down.'" They took him up on the offer and soon he and his friends were in Manchester to see Oasis play. "We had a day out with Manchester, and for me, being from a small village, having a day out in a big city like Manchester was like going to another world," he recalls. "But then to walk out into that stadium . . . " He trails off. "Super Furry Animals was on first and then Oasis came on and it was just electric from that point.

"'The Importance of Being Idle' sounded really, really, really good, but 'Bring It on Down' was incredible, and Oasis hadn't played that one live in god knows how long. I bought any video or DVD they had released at that point, and you'd read gig reviews on the internet and stuff, but they didn't ever play 'Bring It on Down' from *Definitely Maybe*, so I was completely shocked. Wasn't expecting it. And it was such a raw, dirty, gritty rock and roll track. I was just meant to hear that. That's my biggest memories, sound-wise, from that gig."

The gig was a special one, particularly for someone who had waited so long to see them play live. "I'd wanted to do it for, like, ten years. It felt like an eternity. As a twenty-year-old, that was half my life, I'd been wanting to see them," James says. "I'd been wanting to go see them play live for so long. It was electric, or like a film. I was like, 'I finally got here. I've finally done it.' It was just amazing. I had that feeling of like, 'There's my idols on that stage now, seeing them now.' Finally not thinking, 'Will I ever be able to go, will I ever get the opportunity to see them?' and then there I am, in the middle of Manchester, in a huge stadium, watching the best band in the world.

"I've still got pictures on the wall from it. I've got a framed program and tickets done from the day as well," he says. "It was unbelievable, absolutely unbelievable."

The funny thing is that James could have gone to an Oasis show a few years earlier. He knew a girl who had tickets to see Oasis in Newcastle in 2002. "I fancied her at the time and I was begging her to sell me her ticket," James says. "She ended up giving her ticket to her brother because she wanted to hang out with me. A week or two later (after a couple of drinks) I plucked up the courage to ask her out. I grabbed my guitar (that I could barely play) and went to a house where she was babysitting. I tried to play and sing 'Talk Tonight.' That obviously became our song—and it was the song for our first dance at our wedding."

# HALLAM FM ARENA,
## Sheffield,
## February 9–10, 2006

The band's sixth studio album, *Don't Believe the Truth*, came out in 2005 and quickly reached number one on the U.K. album charts and even cracked the top twenty in the U.S. The singles "Lyla" and "The Importance of Being Idle" connected with fans, including many who later named their daughters Lyla.

Fans once again filled arenas to see them play, including George Noble, who didn't really have a say in whether he was going to be an Oasis fan. "It was like the hand-me-down of being an Arsenal fan from my dad, I had no choice. You know, it's like a family require-ment," he says. "My cousins were both at Knebworth, and so was my uncle from the other side of my family. Him and his rugby team were employed to, like, run backpacks of money across the site. Every time a bar would have, say, I don't know, forty or fifty grand, they'd stuff a load of money in these bags, and then these big rugby lads would sort of inconspicuously run the money back to the main area, where they had a big warehouse just full of cash. It sounded like it was very ad hoc. Which sounds about right for Oasis."

While he's seen them six times over their careers thus far, one Sheffield show really stands out. "At the Sheffield gig I was sat at the back, seated as well, and I was like, 'Oh, this is gonna be horrendous,'" he recalls, initially annoyed about the seating arrangement. However, he found a true silver lining to the experience, where being a little separated from the mad crowd, he got to appreciate the band and their musical prowess. "I got to sit there and just enjoy them as if I was watching TV. Like, to sit and critique and really understand and marvel at their prowess and ability and just the magnificence of Oasis. Rather than being like pissed up in the crowd, like hugging all my mates and singing along, I got to delve a bit deeper in the live performance, if that makes sense. It was pretty damn spectacular." Fans in the nosebleed seats at future shows may want to keep that in mind.

As the leader of the hardcore band Your Demise, George is not the most likely Oasis fan, and yet he is an ardent one, and on his most recent tour of Southeast Asia, had his band cover "Bring It on Down" at their recent gigs. "We were planning to cover the song before the Oasis shows got announced. It was spooky. It was, like, a fortnight later, the reunion got announced, and they were playing shows across the U.K. and across the world," he says. "And it was like, 'Well, do we still do it now?' Because it seemed a bit beggy, like, 'Oh, we can't do Oasis.' But I was like, 'Nah, I don't give a fuck.' We had to do it. And it's gone down half a storm for the last couple of weeks on tour."

George sees kindred spirits in the punchy Gallagher brothers. "They did everything unorthodox. They were unapologetically themselves and I think that's an important attribute in hardcore and punk and all of that, right? It's very much like: be real. They said they were the biggest band in the world when they were playing like small little pikey rooms in Manchester. All they ever did was envisage that they would be more and more and more and more. Play Knebworth, tour the world, try and break America, finally break America," he states.

"They were just working class, they were just everything that the country needed at the time. They showed the world that all you need to do is pick up a guitar and just be who you are, really. Just be yourself and don't write for anyone other than what you feel, what you like, what strikes chords to you, what makes your heart beat, what makes your pulse race," he says. "They were so confident and so arrogant, but that arrogance was justified, you know? I think that the reality of it is, is that they're like nothing else."

# PALACIO DE LOS DEPORTES,
## Mexico City,
## March 31, 2006

Juan Sanchez was on the night bus from Guadalajara to Mexico City. It wasn't particularly comfortable, but he didn't mind it, because he was going to see his favorite band play at the Palacio de los Deportes. "My good friend, Eduardo, he got tickets for it because it aligned with the weeks that I was staying there, so he got an extra ticket," says Juan. "It was great to take that bus. They stopped at a hotel on each end, and the fare includes breakfast at the hotel when you arrived. So the hotel in Mexico City was amazing. The breakfast was amazing. The one going back home, though, wasn't that good." It was all worth it to see Oasis play the final show of their tour in support of their 2005 album, *Don't Believe the Truth*.

Juan, who grew up in Mexico City, had fallen for the band when he was fifteen and heard *(What's the Story) Morning Glory?* thanks to his friend Raul's little brother. "He went straight for 'Don't Look Back in Anger' and he just played me the song. He was really excited about it because he had heard that the song kind of sounds like 'Imagine' by John Lennon. He was so cute about it. He played me the whole song. By the end of the song, I asked him for his guitar, because I had figured out how to play it."

Oasis was a natural fit for Juan's musical taste, which was formed on a deep love of the Beatles. "I grew up watching *A Hard Day's Night*, the film by the Beatles. I knew the film by heart, and it was actually helping me learn English," he explains. He got a copy of *Morning Glory* and then *Definitely Maybe*. "I remember buying *Definitely Maybe*, the original release only has eleven songs, but in Mexico, they added 'Whatever' as a closing number, so there are twelve tracks on the original Mexican CD," he says. "That song, to me . . . I listened to it on repeat, on repeat, on repeat; just the way it was made, the way it sounds, it was like some light was coming out of it." He needed to go deeper. "There used to be an outdoor market—I don't know if they still have it or not—and there was a guy that had a tent selling bootleg cassettes. And I don't know how he was able to manage to get bootleg Oasis shows, radio performances, shows in many different places, but he did. So I used to buy those," he explains.

He became a lifelong fan of the band, seeing them in Mexico City and later when he moved to Los Angeles. That's also where he met Liam and guitarist Gem Archer. "There's this pub called the Olde King's Head that a lot of English people go to, because they had English fare and all that. And my ex-wife used to work there and her sister used to work there. I was visiting them close to the end of the shift and one of them was like, 'Oh, you know the guys from Oasis are up at the front,' and I was like, 'What?' Got really excited. Nobody had an iPhone, they didn't really exist back then. So I went out to buy an instant camera and asked Liam if I could take a photograph. He was so nice, but I was so starstruck. I could have invited him for a pint. I just bumbled my words. I couldn't say anything to him."

Juan's love of the band continued when he moved to Chicago, which is where he stumbled into a group of fellow fans.

"I used to work at this place called Longman & Eagle. I was a good patron before becoming a bartender there," he explains. One night while he was working there, he started chatting with his coworker James Deia, who saw the band at the Rosemont Horizon in 1996 among other times, and they realized they both liked Oasis. "As a joke he said, 'We should do an Oasis cover band,' and I said, 'That sounds great,'" Juan says. "We kept talking about it, and one of the regulars suggested the name. She said, 'Why don't you call it Broasis?' And we're like, 'Actually, that's not that bad.'" They formed the band with some other friends and coworkers ("Every single person in the band used to work at that place"). They started practicing in 2014, but didn't play a show until 2019, and have been doing it ever since, playing around Chicago and Kansas City, regaling fellow fans with their takes on classic Oasis tunes. For Juan, the music and the friendships it inspired are the perfect complement to his love of the band. He says, "It's ironic that a band that split up because of situations between the brothers, between the two main members who couldn't get along, has brought me my most lasting relationships with friends."

# WAMU THEATER,
## Seattle, Washington,
## August 26, 2008

Oasis started the first leg of their North American tour in support of their seventh album, 2008's *Dig Out Your Soul*, in Seattle. The plan was to zip across Canada and then return to the U.S. later in the year, including gigs in Los Angeles, Auburn Hills, Michigan, and finally playing at Madison Square Garden. They didn't know, of course, that it was to be their last tour of North America for seventeen years.

Greg Glover, the morning-show host at alternative radio station 94.7 KNRK FM in Portland, Oregon, had big plans for the Seattle show. It's about a three-hour drive north, and he was dragging a lot of friends up with him. "I bought ten tickets with my own money, and gathered all of my friends, because I was like, 'You have to see them with me.' We all traveled up together. I just wanted it to be an event," he says. "I still really liked them. I actually really got back into them with their [2005] album *Don't Believe the Truth*, which may be my favorite Oasis record."

While he loved the music, the shows were a little underwhelming. "It was at the WAMU Theater, which is a really boring venue. It's kind of like seeing a band play at a convention center. It was really lame," he says. "And then the next night I drove up to Canada, and the show was somewhere in Vancouver, BC, and they played the same exact set, the same both nights. I mean, to be honest with you, seeing them in a big arena certainly wasn't like seeing them at, you know, Wetlands, that's for sure."

By that point in 2008, Greg was pretty ride-or-die with the band, anyway. "We stuck with them even when they weren't popular. I mean, god forbid, I even tried to find a reason to like *Standing on the Shoulder of Giants* and my friend Arty [Shepherd, who saw them at Wetlands and the Stone Pony] was like, 'No, you got to listen to *Heathen Chemistry*,'" he says, laughing. "I kind of stuck with them because they were kind of out of fashion at that point, but, you know, I'm a dedicated guy, and just stuck with them through thick and thin. I felt like I owed it to them for some reason."

He felt loyal to Oasis, because like a lot of Oasis fans, he saw himself in the Gallaghers. "'Morning Glory' is still a song that, when I hear it, it makes me want to put my fist through a wall, in a good way. I love it. I loved their story," he says. "I'm a Southerner. I'm from a little town called Hueytown, Alabama. I was raised by a single mom. I had jerk stepdads. We didn't have much growing up, so I really resonated with the Gallaghers and their story. I don't know. Maybe it's the fact that, you know, Northerners in England are kind of like Southerners in the U.S., and they're sometimes dismissed. And I liked the fact that they grew up with next to nothing, too, and were working class. I really identified with that."

While Greg works in music and is surrounded by new bands, new records, new videos every day, Oasis holds a very special place in his heart and always will. "Oasis might be the last band I truly loved and worshipped," he says. "I don't think I've loved a band like that since them, you know? They don't exist anymore."

# TORONTO ISLAND PARK,
## Toronto,
## September 7, 2008

Oasis was in the middle of the *Dig Out Your Soul* tour when they swung back through Toronto to play Virgin Festival, a two-day musical festival on the Toronto Islands. Fans were excited to see Oasis headline, particularly because the Jam's Paul Weller was also playing the festival. The hope—and rumor—was that he would join Oasis onstage to reprise the guitar riffs he played while recording the original "Champagne Supernova." That never happened because Noel Gallagher was attacked in the middle of the show.

"I was actually shooting," says photographer and Oasis superfan Lisa Mark, who first saw them at the Maple Leaf Gardens in 1998. "I had been in the pit a few minutes before, and when it happened, it was a few songs in, during 'Morning Glory,' if I recall. We were up in the VIP area with our friends after I had been shooting, and the band is just playing like normal, and then all of a sudden, you see this guy rush the stage and take out Noel. He just went down like a ton of bricks. It was terrifying."

A man, later determined to be forty-eight-year-old Daniel Sullivan, had jumped onstage and headed straight for Noel, knocking him down. The audience had no idea what they were witnessing. "It was just really upsetting," says Lisa. "We didn't know if he had been stabbed. We didn't know what had happened. It all happened so darn fast. And then Liam went after the guy. I think he was just shocked. I mean, we all were, but he kind of waited, he hesitated before he went for the guy. I think it was just because he didn't process what just happened, either, you know? Then all of a sudden you see the security teams and the managers and, like, everybody's just running out from the side, tackling the guy, and then Liam's coming at him, like, 'I'm gonna kick your ass!' It was really upsetting at the time. I just remember being so shocked. I was almost in tears. It was a very visceral reaction."

Everyone left the stage, and the crowd had no idea what to do. "An announcer came out and he was talking, like, 'Okay, we gotta figure out what's going on here,'" continues Lisa. "I remember there was another photographer in the pit, and they got photos of the actual attack as the guy was shoving him. I just remember they were so excited. And like half of me, I understand catching the moment, but the other half of me, I got ragey angry at the photographer. I actually yelled at them, because I was so mad that they were so excited. We literally didn't know if Noel had been stabbed, or something, at that point. We didn't know how serious it was. I'm talking literally in the moment, the photographer was like, 'Look what I got! Look what I got!' And I'm like, 'That's fine, but this man might be hurt.'"

After Oasis left the stage to tend to Noel, the crowd wasn't really expecting them to return. However, the band eventually did, and even finished the show, much to the thrill of the audience. "It was just euphoria, everybody got right back into the gig, and then it was a great gig," she says. "But the whole time I'm sitting there, thinking, 'Is he okay?'"

Lisa and her husband, Justin, had met Noel's security earlier, as they were all staying at the same hotel, and asked him about the attack. "He goes, 'Oh man, Noel is mad. He's very mad.' I don't blame him at all, but yeah, Noel's apparent reaction was just anger. But he went through it like a champ, like a professional. I think he was in shock, but he rode it out."

Once he returned to the stage to finish the show, Lisa snapped a few more photos. "You can see in those photos that Noel's face, he's

in pain," she says. "He ended up having broken ribs and they had to cancel their next shows."

The attacker pleaded guilty to assault. Oasis was meant to finish their tour at New York City's Terminal 5, but the show was canceled as Noel recovered from his injuries. They returned to the stage a month later in Liverpool.

# MAKUHARI MESSE,
## Tokyo,
## March 28–29, 2009

ack in 1994, just a month after *Definitely Maybe* was released, before Oasis ever toured in the U.S., the boys were put onto a plane to Japan. They played four nights at Shibuya Club Quattro in Tokyo, followed by dates in Osaka and Nagoya. The response was rapid and rabid. Videos and photos taken during their tour show the band members mobbed by fans in their hotels and at the gigs. It was like Beatlemania, now starring five lads from Manchester.

Subsequent visits featured sold-out shows in arenas nationwide, including three sold-out nights at the famed Budokan venue in 1998. Thanks to countless TV appearances, liberal use of their music in commercials, the selection of an Oasis track as the theme song to a popular anime, and dozens of tour dates around the country, plus, of course, the international appeal of the band's music, their popularity in Japan has barely waned over the years. Oasis even paid tribute to their ardent fan base in the East in the "Acquiesce" music video, which features an Asian cover band playing the song in front of an all-Asian crowd.

When Oasis returns to Tokyo for two nights during the reunion tour, members of O+asis, Japan's best Oasis tribute band (a self-proclaimed title), will be in the audience to see their idols perform. O+asis performs regularly around Tokyo to any fans who miss Oasis, missed Oasis, or just miss hearing their favorite songs played live. "It's mainly Japanese people who listened to Oasis in the 1990s and 2000s," says twenty-six-year-old Kazuhito Shinohara, the lead singer of the cover band. "There are also enthusiastic people who find us on the internet and come to see the gig from abroad." Kazu, like many other younger fans around the world, fell in love with Oasis through You-Tube, specifically watching the performance of "Live Forever" from the 1996 Maine Road show. Fittingly, O+asis puts most of their shows on YouTube and shares the content across social media, finding new young fans for their spin on Oasis tunes. "People from all over the world, including Japan, are happy to send messages. Of course, there are people who listen to us in real time, but I'm happy that there are young people there, too," says Kaoru Ueda, the forty-five-year-old guitarist in the group. He also fell in love with the band online after watching one live performance. "It was 'Wonderwall,' which my brother showed me (though Liam wasn't there, LOL). I immediately borrowed an acoustic guitar from a friend and started playing it," he recalls. Kaoru was lucky enough to see Oasis headline the Fuji Rock Festival in 2001, his first music festival, when they stopped by on their *Standing on the Shoulder of Giants* tour. Now, after years of playing Noel in the cover band, he will be at the reunion show to see his idols again.

Also in the crowd will be Shotaro Nishida. Shotaro has seen Oasis once before, at Makuhari Messe in Tokyo in 2009. He was there with his brother, two friends, and a bandmate, and they had arrived at the show early. "I wanted to see them live at the front of the show," he notes.

"The first song of the live show was 'Rock 'n' Roll Star' and it brought tears to my eyes!" he recalls. The sold-out crowd stood for the duration of the show and occasionally got a little out of control, not that Shotaro minded. "The crowd were all crazy fans!" he remembers. "Some people in the audience got violent and I felt I had to protect myself, which I felt was a danger to myself, but I also felt that this was part of the greatness of the live performance of the band Oasis."

Seeing the band he loved live was an incredible experience for him. "It didn't seem real that they were right there in front of me," he says. "It was like watching a DVD. That's how special it was for me!"

While they were able to be near the front, they weren't able to find time to get any merch. The memories were better than T-shirts anyway, although Shotaro is a self-professed fashion lover, particularly when it comes to Oasis style. "I'm a Liam Gallagher fanatic, so I love collecting the same clothes he wears," he states. "I spend all my money on my collection."

When Oasis returns to Tokyo, Shotaro will once again be in the audience with his brother, but now he feels even more connected to the band. "I am in a band called SAHAJi with my brother," he explains. Their forthcoming album is being produced by Nick Brine, the recording engineer who worked behind the boards on both *(What's the Story?) Morning Glory?* and *Be Here Now.* "I've always had a connection with Oasis!" says Shotaro. The full album will be released this year and the band will be touring the U.K., the U.S., and Japan.

# ESTADIO NACIONAL DEL PERÚ,
## Lima,
## April 30, 2009

While Oasis had been steadily touring the world since 1994, it wasn't until 1998 that they first headed to South America as part of the *Be Here Now* tour. The performance at the Estadio San Carlos de Apoquindo in Santiago, Chile, was captured on film for *Live at Apoquindo Stadium*, and despite the fact that Liam's voice is straining, the stadium is packed and the crowd is rapturous. It was a scene that was repeated at stops in Argentina, over two dates in Brazil, and finally in Mexico City, where each venue was filled with ardent fans singing along to every word in English. Oasis returned to Argentina and Brazil in 2001, and played in Venezuela as well, during the *Standing on the Shoulder of Giants* tour.

It's their 2009 show at the River Plate stadium in Buenos Aires that has become legendary among fans, though. Not because of the band exactly, but because of the crowd. During "Don't Look Back in Anger," Noel tells the crowd to feel free to sing along, and the response is so overwhelming and beautiful that there are whole Reddit threads dedicated to it. Noel doesn't even bother trying to sing, just letting the euphoric crowd pour out the words back to the man who wrote them. The video has racked up millions of views on You-Tube from fans around the globe wanting to watch an ephemeral performance captured on camera. "When I am feeling low—and I mean *low*—I listen to that song at River Plate, to that crowd coming together and singing," says Josh Isaacs, a Zambian fan of the band. "There is no truer expression of love than when a crowd takes the spotlight away from the band. If I was an artist, to hear a crowd do that? Just wow." Isaacs has yet to see Oasis perform live, as the band performed in Africa only twice, both times in South Africa. However, like countless other fans around the world, he fell in love with the band online through the music and the concert footage, particularly through that performance at River Plate. While the performance at that Argentinian soccer stadium has gone down in the history books for fans, a few nights before there was a show in Lima, Perú, that Carlos Medina argues was even better.

Carlos was a college student in Lima in 1994 when he heard a song on the radio and had to know who it was. "I was about to go to the university, but I returned to my home to phone the radio station and asked, 'Who's that band?' And they told me it was Oasis," he recalls. Carlos already had "Live Forever" and "Supersonic" on a loop, and *Definitely Maybe* on cassette, but it was the strings on the end of "Whatever" that caught his attention that day, and the new sound made him fall in love with the band. It wasn't until 1995 that he got to see what the band looked like, though. "We didn't have cable TV here in Perú, but there was a music program on a local TV station, and they showed the 'Roll with It' video, and I said, 'Oh, *that* is Oasis,'" he remembers. Carlos had been studying

English for several years when he first heard the band, but found that listening to them helped hone his language skills. "The lyrics of Oasis helped me to improve my vocabulary, because it was a different English," he notes. "I learned American English, and this was a British English."

He didn't get to see his ersatz language tutors live until 2001, when Oasis brought their *Standing on the Shoulder of Giants* tour to Buenos Aires to play at the Hot Festival with Neil Young. "I was, like, twenty-three years old. I was in my first job, so I got the money, I got the vacation, and I traveled to Argentina with a friend of mine who is also a fan," he says. "It was the first time and it was amazing, unbelievable. And after that I saw them in 2006, also in Buenos Aires, and then in 2009 here in Perú, when they played at our national stadium."

The one and only time Oasis played in Lima, during the *Dig Out Your Soul* tour, stands out to Carlos, not just because he didn't have to travel to Argentina, but because of the fierce fandom that he saw on display at the show. "I think the concert in Lima was much more intense than the one at River Plate," he avers. "But obviously they showed the pro-shot video from River Plate, because there was no professionally shot video in Lima." The fans showed up early, according to Carlos: "Everybody went to the airport, a lot of people, like one or two thousand people at the airport to meet them, and then at the hotel, too."

When it came time for the sold-out show, fans came out in force. "The National Stadium was full, like fifty thousand people, and it was amazing for me as a fan, because I hadn't realized that there was so many fans of Oasis here in Perú. There were a lot of people at that concert, and for me, it was amazing, because I was almost in the front row, and when Noel played 'Don't Look Back in Anger' and everybody started singing, I just turned around to the stadium to watch. It was amazing to see everybody with the cell phones lit up and all that. It was a pretty, pretty good image for me."

These days Carlos devotes his free time to hosting *Whatever: El Podcast De Oasis En Español,* and in that capacity has spent a lot of time thinking about Oasis fandom in South America. He thinks there are so many passionate Oasis fans in South America because people there, like nearly everywhere else in the world, connect with the band's origin story. "I think we can relate to the story of these working-class kids that became famous from nowhere, from nothing," Carlos says. "I think it's the same dream for us. You know, this region, South America, is very rich in resources, but we are not very rich people because we have a pretty crap governance. That's the difference. And we dream about being famous, we dream about being something like Oasis. We can relate to the story of these working-class kids that became famous, and that's why we love them very much—also we have an admiration for good-looking people."

While Oasis sings in English, Carlos believes the music is powerful enough to cross language barriers. "The music speaks for itself, you know?" he claims. "I know there are so many people that don't understand what they are singing about, but I can feel and I can see the emotion when they sing it, the emotion in the particular words. So I think it's more than the words, it is the feeling of the music, what that music can transmit to you, to your soul. You receive the message, but not in words, but as a whole."

While Oasis is not returning to Lima on their reunion tour, they will be back at River Plate, and once again Carlos will be heading to Buenos Aires, undoubtedly comparing crowds, but thrilled to be there among his fellow fans.

# HEATON PARK,
## Manchester,
## July 4–7, 2009

Hannah Shillito was excited to bring her friend to see Oasis play on their home turf at Heaton Park in Manchester. She had been a fan of the band since she was twelve years old and her dad bought her *Definitely Maybe* as a birthday present. "It was kind of like a real bonding thing for my dad and I," Hannah says. "He's not a very emotional man. He's from the north of England. He doesn't talk about his feelings. So how he expressed his love and bonded with me was through music, and he just got me that album. I just remember hearing it the first time and going, 'Oh my god, what is this? It's amazing.' And then I just fell in love, and I've been in love ever since. And now I'm forty-one."

She had seen the band perform live before, when Oasis stopped in Bolton to play two sold-out nights at the Reebok Stadium during their *Standing on the Shoulder of Giants* tour. Bolton is near Manchester and it very much felt like a hometown show. "I was supposed to go with my dad, but my dad got really ill. We nearly lost him, actually, and he couldn't go," Hannah recalls. "I remember going with my best friend from school. It wasn't quite the same, because I wanted to be there with my dad, obviously, but my dad was insistent that I go. And it was . . . I can't even describe it. It was ridiculously amazing, like just being able to see them in the flesh. And I think because it was near where they're from—and they're where I'm from, as well, and I know they have worldwide fans, but if you're from the same place as them, you sort of get them a bit more. Do you know what I mean? Like, you're in tune with their little mannerisms and their little sayings, and you like what they like, and you get the little idioms. So it was just amazing being surrounded by people who genuinely loved them as well. All the blokes had haircuts like them, too—all of them—it was like a sea of Gallagher brothers."

Hannah has gone to many Oasis shows over the years, but they've all had one thing in common: "I've only ever seen them up north, on their own home turf," she says. "That added meaning. That added extra, because they always get really excited about being back home as well."

When she saw that the band was coming to another iconic Manchester venue, she bought tickets and asked a friend to join her. There was just one wee problem. "I remember going with one of my friends, who's from the south of England, and I said to him, 'You need to wear a rain jacket because they will throw pints of urine at you,'" Hannah remembers, laughing.

"I don't know why, but I just get so excited at these shows that I'm like, 'It's a thing that we just have to accept it.' And he was like, 'That's absolutely disgusting.' And I was like, 'I know, but you just have to get into it, because that's just what happens. I don't know! Just go with it, because they can do whatever they want.' It's awful, isn't it?" Hannah cracks up laughing recalling this. "I've never thrown one myself, but I have to say I have had one thrown at me. And the thing is—I don't care! I don't care, because I love them so much. I don't care!"

So over the course of attending Oasis shows on their home turf, she has learned to wear a poncho and be prepared to go home and shower after a show. For Hannah, though, it's all worth the cost of admission to see her beloved band up close. "If you're gonna get right in amongst it, then you're going to just have to suck it up; not literally, but you're going to have to just go with it. You're just so high from, like, the music and the crowd and the atmosphere and the feelings from listening to your favorite songs that you don't think about that. You don't care, honestly," she says. "And I'm a nice person, I promise! It's not like I go throwing wee around, but I don't care when I'm at an Oasis gig, I do not care."

Hannah believes that this particular concert activity wasn't as prevalent at early gigs, but is a bit of a hallmark at later ones. Another fan mentioned being at Wembley and noticing lads, pretty much always lads, posting up in a spot, drinking pint after pint after pint, and then not wanting to leave to use the loo and risk losing their space, so they pee in a cup. It almost makes sense. The throwing-it-up-in-the-air part is a bit of a mystery. "Whoever started it, well, somebody needs to have a word with them. It's horrible," says Hannah, shooing one of her kids out the door. "But you love Oasis so much that you tolerate it."

———

As a young kid living in Manchester in the early nineties, there was no choice but to be an Oasis fan. "Everybody kind of knew about the boys from Burnage that just been signed, but I was only a young lad then, so you couldn't go to the gigs. All you could do is copy the haircut and buy a CD," says Kyle Dale. While his brother went to see them at Maine Road, Kyle had to wait until the 10 Years of Noise tour in 2001 to see them for the first time. However, it was their last show at Heaton Park in 2009 that he really remembers. "It was right before they broke up, which coincidentally was my first date with my current wife. Current wife? My *only* wife," he says, laughing. "I've got a print downstairs that [artist] Pete McKee gave to me after that gig that was signed by all the band. It's just a beautiful, rare piece," he says. According to Kyle, his home is filled with beautiful, rare pieces. It makes sense, as he is one of the country's—if not the world's—biggest dealers in band memorabilia and merchandise and many of his favorite items are on display in his house. "I mean, it's not an Oasis shrine like the Alan Partridge sketch. It's all bands," he clarifies, but he does love "watching people's faces as they go from room to room going, 'Wow.'"

His collecting started innocently enough. He was living in Scotland and homesick. "I was missing home. I've had a whiskey, I'm on eBay, let's see what I can buy. Vinyl wasn't ridiculously priced then, so I got into buying all the singles and the albums, and then the box sets, and then I got into looking at other promo items and whatnot. And it ended up being, I've got the stage kit from Knebworth with the Man City logo next to me, and Noel's guitars around." He then started buying and selling items and working with other collectors to buy and sell *their* items. "I was able to cherry-pick the items I wanted to keep for me, sell the rest, and get the money back and make a profit," he explains. "I was doing that and building a reputation for being a trusted source."

Kyle worked as a financial advisor for fifteen years, traveling the country for his job, but a health crisis led him to reassess. "I got cancer, unfortunately, twice, and that kind of knocked me back a little bit," he says. "Obviously, I survived. I'm not a ghost." After facing down those two rounds of cancer he was looking for something new to do that would keep him closer to his three little kids. "I had a drunken chat with the missus one night and said, 'Look, this passion of collecting that I've had over the years has sort of turned into a little business because of all the deals that are going around and the money that's moving. I think we could turn this into something.'" He now runs a company called Bittersweet Home, where he buys, sells, trades, and authenticates band merchandise and memorabilia. He runs a Facebook group for Oasis collectors and puts on Q&A panels and plans events and exhibitions to display the merchandise and memorabilia. Every event he does has a charitable angle, too. He recently put on an event and exhibition for the Manchester rec center, Salford Lads Club, which famously served as a backdrop for a photo of the Smiths. The club has been in dire financial straits and was recently threatened with closure. The event helped raise £17,000 in two days. "They were, like, in tears," says Kyle. "That's the proud moment, not the exhibition going well."

He has seen Oasis five or so times, but expects to quadruple that, as he is following the band as they tour both the U.K. and the U.S. during their reunion shows. He isn't just being a groupie, though; he is running an exhibition of Oasis memorabilia that will follow the tour and give fans a chance to see some rare items collected over the course of the band's long career. The prize in his collection, though, won't be on display: a digital audiotape, or DAT, containing three unreleased songs from the *Be Here Now* era, all on one little tape. "Two of those songs, if they came out now, the world would stop. They're that good," says Kyle. "They're like prime *Masterplan* acoustic Noel era." Kyle was offered a great deal of money for them, but instead held on to them until he could get them back to Noel. "It took four years until I finally got them back in his hand," he says. "Now I'm hoping they'll be released as official, unheard *Be Here Now* B-side tracks."

# V FESTIVAL,
## Weston Park, U.K.,
## August 23, 2009

When David Blurton—Blurt to his friends—walked onto the V Festival grounds in Chelmsford, he was expecting to hit a big milestone—his fiftieth Oasis concert. The band was slated to headline the festival. They had played the V Festival in Weston Park the night before and were supposed to take the stage again at Chelmsford. They never did.

David grew up in Capel St. Mary, a tiny village in Suffolk, where it was hard to discover new music. Then one day, he flipped on the stereo and heard something wholly different. "It just blew my mind, basically, and just sent me on a mad thirty-odd-year trip," he says, laughing. "The obsession probably started around Christmas of '94, when they released 'Whatever.'" He was hooked and went out to find their album. "I bought Snoop's *Doggystyle* and *Definitely Maybe* on the same day," he says. "Obviously, two very, massively different genres of music, but bought both on the same day, on CDs, and even to this day, they're still two of my favorite albums."

It was Oasis, though, that really took hold of him. "I suppose being in quite a rural setting, not a lot going on, and then you hear these angry young men from Manchester City, and they're just speaking about everyday life," he says. "It just really resonated with me at the time. Just being able to be free, being able to do whatever you want to do, being a rock and roll star, metaphorically, really it just allowed me to believe in dreams, I guess. And then throughout my teenage years, and also into my adult life, just every time there was a problem or a situation, it just seemed to be a lyric or a song that fit. Knowing that there were other people that had experienced this just kind of helped."

He started collecting the bootlegs on CDs. "At one point, it was probably a world-class collection," he says. The first time he saw them live was at Earls Court in 1995, and that kick-started a drive to see them over and over again, which, of course, included Knebworth. "That was the most hectic experience," he says. "Those tickets went on sale at something like eight o'clock in the morning, and obviously it was landlines, pre-mobile, and we had this home phone attached to the wall by the front door, and basically I had a seat by the front door, calling and redialing all the time. It was FA Cup Final day in the U.K.. I think I got the tickets as the teams walked out to the pitch. So obviously everyone would have given up hope or whatever and just decided to watch the football. So that would have been about three o'clock. So from eight until three, I was just constantly redialing."

The Knebworth gig was as incredible as he had hoped. He was seventeen, and watching his favorite band in a crowd of people who also loved them. "The buzz when 'Columbia' started was absolutely incredible," he said. "I think loving a band is a bit like loving a football team, right? Like you support them, and you'll go through the ups and downs with them," he says, looking back now at the age of forty-five. "And it was just this coming together of people who felt exactly the same way as yourself, just this real affinity. It was a good time to be young, just a really good time to be young."

Of course, being young, he needed a little help getting rides to and from shows. "We had arranged to meet my father to pick us up after the concert," he says, chuckling at the innocence of it all. "Obviously, I had no comprehension of the vast number of people who would actually be there. So we'd arranged to meet my dad at Knebworth train station, and obviously, there were two hundred fifty thousand other people trying to meet someone at Knebworth train station. This was all prior to the days of mobile phones. Then we literally bumped into him in the crowd. So that was amazing, honestly. We turned around and just bumped into someone, and it happened to be him. So luckily, we got the lift home."

David went on to see Oasis dozens more times, watching their Wembley Stadium debut in 2000, going to shows around the U.K. and across Europe, and traveling as far as Berlin to see them run through their catalog live. Eventually he had seen them forty-nine times and was set to hit the fiftieth-show milestone at the V Festival in Chelmsford. Not that he was counting, exactly, he just wanted to see them play. "I wasn't going because it was my fiftieth, if that makes sense. I was just going to the show, and it just happened to be the fiftieth," he says. "It was never like, 'I need to see them X amount of times.' It was never an ambition I needed to achieve."

So on August 23, 2009, David headed to Chelmsford. The lineup included the Killers, Dizzee Rascal, and a rising star called Lady Gaga. Oasis was set to take the stage last, and David, who was "drunk and happy," was sitting on the grass waiting. And waiting. Then Snow

Patrol came on instead and it became clear that Oasis wasn't going to play that day. It was announced that Liam had laryngitis. The band was scheduled to play at Rock en Seine in Paris a few days later, but the set was canceled "as a result of an altercation within the band." Oasis had broken up. They wouldn't play together again for a decade and a half. Until their reunion shows fifteen years later, many fans thought they would never play again.

If all goes according to plan, David will finally hit the fiftieth-show milestone at Wembley Stadium.

He's already thinking about making Tokyo his fifty-first.

# PART IV

# THE IN-BETWEEN DAYS –

## PRESENT

# THE IN-BETWEEN DAYS

Oasis broke up after a big dustup backstage at the Rock en Seine festival. While only the two brothers really know what happened, it has been reported that Liam may have thrown a plum, followed by a guitar, and maybe Noel smashed a guitar in retaliation. What was clear was that Noel was done. He issued a statement saying that he "simply could not go on working with Liam a day longer." And that was the end of Oasis, at least at the time. While everyone thought the band was done for good, they eventually reunited. The guitar also wasn't a lost cause.

Philippe Dubreuille had a little guitar shop on Denmark Street and started working with Oasis when one of Andy Bell's guitars was broken on tour and they asked him to repair it. "That was kind of a magic work, because no one could see it, you know?" Philippe says. "And they've been pleased with that." He customized their guitars, added a smoky sunburst to one of Noel's Gibsons, repaired what was broken, made a guitar for Gem Archer and another for Andy Bell. So when Noel's red Gibson 355 was smashed in France, he's the guy they called.

"They have that fight in Paris, you know, and Liam broke one guitar of Noel's. Noel broke one guitar of Liam's, and from that day for fifteen years, they never reformed," says Philippe. "I don't think Noel even knew I was going to do it. They used to have a guy, his name was Jason Rhodes, who was the roadie of Noel. He made the decision, and had been bringing the guitar to many guitar makers around in England, and they would say, 'Oh, that guitar? No, it's fucked.' Okay. You can say, get the insurance and all of that. And Jason brought the guitar to me, and said, 'Do you think you could repair that guitar?' Let's say, 'Yeah, leave it with me,' and all of that. And after one month, I've done a really meticulous job. You could never see the guitar has been broken. It was like magic. Everybody was stunned and said, 'Wow, shit,' and all, that it was incredible. But Noel, I'm not sure that he was so happy that Jason made the decision to bring the guitar. Because maybe for him it means, 'Okay, this is the end of Oasis, so leave it like that.' But in another way he was really pleased. And Noel, apparently, he was not playing that guitar and he sold it to a French guy."

———

While rumors of a reunion swirled off and on for years, when news broke in 2024 that the shows were really being scheduled, one person took a little pride in feeling he may have played a small role: Nick Harmer, the best bass player on the planet. "I can't take all the credit for the Oasis reunion, but I can claim that I was doing my part to run a black-ops campaign to move the needle in that direction," he explains. "Back in March of 2023, [my band] Death

Cab for Cutie was on a European tour and we had a day off in Manchester. We were staying in a downtown hotel, but our tour bus was parked nearby. I had run out to the bus to retrieve my phone charger, and as I was stepping back off the bus a group of Manchester lads happened to be walking by. I could see they were immediately curious about who was stepping off the bus, but I could also see they had exactly zero idea of who I was. Still, though, they were curious, and one of them stepped forward and asked, 'Whose bus is this?' Now, one thing I've learned is you can convince a lot of people of a lot of things if you're just stepping off a tour bus when you say it. I don't know why it came to me so quickly, but without hesitation I lowered my voice and stepped closer. 'Can you boys keep a secret?' I asked. I could see their interest pique when they heard my American accent. 'I've been flown in to Manchester to help with the Oasis reunion rehearsals.' Their eyes widened and mouths dropped open. 'You're joking.' I doubled down. 'They don't want anyone to know yet, but they're back together and rehearsing here in Manchester right now.' My confidence and American accent sealed the deal. I turned, and I felt like the slo-mo guy walking away from the explosion as I left them all standing there in shock and awe. Mouths agape. True believers. I could only hope they went and immediately called everyone they knew in town. And maybe, just maybe, the rumor would pick up enough steam to find its way back to one of the Gallagher brothers and they'd think, 'Fuck, if it's a rumor already, we might as well do it for real.'"

Marco Collins also felt like he played a role in getting the band back together. Marco was the music director and nighttime host of a station in Seattle called 107.9 The End, all throughout the nineties. It was his radio station that helped turn under-the-radar artists like Nirvana, Beck, Weezer, and Pearl Jam into household names. He was honored by the Rock & Roll Hall of Fame for his efforts. He was also an early supporter of Oasis after browsing in a record shop when he was in England for the Reading Festival. "I went to the record store, and the first thing I found was the 'Live Forever' CD single. I just remember falling in love with it, and it's still today my favorite Oasis song," he says. "I just remember getting that in England, thinking, 'Holy shit, I can't wait to bring this home to the States.'

"I remember playing it, and I remember getting a great response from it, because it was different," he says. "It was still a rock song, but it definitely had that melodic side of things, harmonies and just the hook of that song that captures people."

When Oasis kick-started their first U.S. tour in Seattle at Moe's Mo' Rockin' Café in 1994, Marco was there. "I think I even introduced that show," he says. So he had history with the band, and cred, and was also just a big fan of Noel. "I'm a fan of his songwriting," he says. "Liam's got a fucking fantastic voice, but I've always been a Noel guy. I love his solo stuff."

When Marco found out Noel was coming to town in June 2023, he asked for an interview for his radio show at 98.9 KPNW, but Noel's "management turned me down," Marco says. "It was the first night of the tour, and, you know, he wasn't getting a ton of radio play at that time and they turned me down." Marco doesn't really like taking no for an answer, though. "I kind of went back to them and asked them to reconsider," he says. "I've known Noel. I've interviewed him many times. So they reconsidered. They asked Noel if he would do the interview, and he said yes, but they told me, 'Do not ask him about Oasis. Don't ask him about his brother.'" Marco was okay with that. At least he said he was when he agreed to it.

"I did the interview with Noel. I got through to the end of the interview, and it was fantastic. I really loved his record. I thought it was just so good, and if some of those songs were Oasis songs, I think they would have been huge. So we got on fantastic, he remembered me, which was awesome, and then at the end, well . . . "

What had happened was that Liam had started a tiny war online. "Three days before the interview, Liam went online, went on Twitter, and was slamming Noel and talking all kinds of shit about getting the band back together. I can't remember exactly what Liam posted, but it had pissed Noel off, and it was everywhere," Marco recalls. As a journalist with direct access to the artist and no one to really stop him, Marco decided to go right to the source. "I was like, 'I'm going for it. We're getting along so well. He's in such a good mood.' So I sunk my teeth in and asked him about Liam and whether or not the band would ever get back together. At that point, I had no idea what kind of response I would get out of him. I was ready for it to be shot down."

Marco wasn't sure whether Noel would walk out, say something biting, or just glare at him. Instead, he seized the opportunity to call out his little brother. "Noel not only took the bait, he went hard," Marco says. "I mean, he looked into the camera, pointed at the camera, and said, 'I dare you. I dare you to call me.' He launched into this tirade."

Here's how it went. Marco asked about Liam's tweets and then pushed a little more to ask about whether there was a chance of an Oasis reunion. "He's gonna have to call me. He's going to have to get someone to call me because he's been going on about it for the last fucking ten, or whatever it is," Noel said. "He doesn't want it and he knows that neither of us is particularly fucking interested in it. I know he doesn't want it, and I'm very comfortable in what I do. I couldn't give a flying fuck one way or the other. But he keeps going on about it and I'm like, 'Well, okay. Call us then. Let's see what you've got to say.'"

Noel then pointed at the camera. "I dare him," he said. "If you're watching this now, I assume this is going on YouTube. I fucking dare you to call me. I dare you to call me. And you won't call me because [what] if you do call me and I go, 'Actually that's a good idea.'"

Marco was thrilled. "The entire time it's happening, I'm like, 'Oh shit, this is gold. This is gonna go viral,'" he recalls. "And so it was funny, when we were done, I said, 'Thanks, Noel,' and I go, 'You know what's gonna happen with this, right?' And he looked at me and just smiled and walked out the door. He knew what he was doing. He knew one hundred percent what he was doing. Once it did go viral and started picking up steam, management asked us to take it down, and I was like, 'I'm not taking that down, no way!' I didn't want to further hurt my relationship with the band, but in reality, even if I had taken it down, it had been shared so many times already, it was so out there, that it wouldn't have made sense."

Marco likes to think that his interview and asking the one question he wasn't supposed to ask helped move things along with the reunion. "I saw an interview where Liam was saying, 'I'm the one that called. I gave in,'" Marco says. "So I'd like to believe that, yeah, I had something to do with that process."

# THE REUNION SHOWS

Fans had been hearing rumblings about something happening with Oasis. Most thought it was going to be a reissue or something having to do with the upcoming anniversary for *Definitely Maybe*. It wasn't that. Two days before *Definitely Maybe*'s anniversary, the band announced that they were getting back together for a series of dates in the United Kingdom and Ireland initially, including shows at Wembley Stadium in London and Heaton Park in Manchester. The fans responded accordingly.

"When the reunion was announced, like last summer, I got people that I went to school with, like, messaging me and going, 'Are you okay?' And I was like, 'I'm not okay, actually,'" says Irish fan Sarah Breen, laughing.

She wasn't alone in that response. The Zwolaks, the Oasis superfans with Oasis license plates and three of Liam's tambourines, were driving from North Carolina back to New York when they stopped at a rest stop in Maryland. "We popped in and Lyla went to the ladies' room and I'm standing there getting some cheese fries or something, and I looked down at my phone, and I'm just like, 'Wait, what?'" says Brian. "I looked at Jen and just said, 'Come here. Come here right now.'"

"The way he looked at me, I thought somebody had passed away," Jennifer adds.

"She walked over and I'm just like, 'Oasis have gotten back together,'" says Brian. "All of a sudden she went completely white, like the rest of the world ceased to exist.

"And then Lyla came out of the ladies' room and she was wearing one of my old T-shirts—my *Live by the Sea* Oasis T-shirts—and that's the vision I have," says Jennifer. "I'm stunned and watching her walking towards me with the T-shirt on and just being like, 'Oh my god.' It was unbelievable."

Brian continues. "Yeah, and we got back in the car and there's Noel—our Noel—sitting there, and we're just like, 'Oh my god,' and I'm trying to calm Jen down because she was hyperventilating."

"It was bad," Jen says, laughing. "I just couldn't believe it. I didn't think that they could affect me the same way they did when I was a teenager and after all those years, and they did."

The Zwolaks got up at 3 a.m. to watch the official announcement of the reunion tour. And they woke up at 3 a.m. again in time to get in the long queue for tickets to the tour. "We are flying over to London for the first Wembley show, July 25," says Brian. "And then we have tickets here for the two shows in New York and the two shows in Toronto and the show in Chicago."

Their kids are going to all of them. "They've never seen Oasis because they weren't born," says Jennifer. "We've just had them brainwashed since the day they were born and that's it."

They do have one warning for the teenagers, though: "I keep telling them, prepare yourself for me to embarrass you," says Jen. "Because it's going to happen."

———

Rasha Al Aqeedi will be seeing Oasis for the first time at the reunion show in New Jersey. She has been an Oasis fan since 1995, but she didn't hear a full album, not a single one, until 2003. That's because she grew up in Saddam Hussein's Iraq and it was pretty much impossible to access the music.

"In Iraq, during the sanctions under Saddam's regime—dictatorship—we didn't have media. We had two TV channels that were fully controlled by the government. From time to time, they would broadcast American or Western movies or music, but it wasn't very consistent. Now, I had spent a portion of my childhood in the United States, so my English was good enough, and I loved pop culture, so I would watch when and what I could." Rasha's father had earned a PhD that was paid for by the Iraqi government on the condition he return and serve his country in some way, and even though Iraq had invaded Kuwait and America was bombing the country, he felt obligated to go back. "A few months after we returned, there was immediate regret, because the sanctions were rough," Rasha recalls.

"When we moved back to Iraq in '92 I became very obsessed with the radio, because that's the one place where I could listen to music," she says. They also had limited TV channels, but in the spring of 1995, when she was eleven, one of those channels started playing the U.K. top fifty every Tuesday. "Take That was number one with 'Back for Good,' and they were there for three weeks, and on the fourth week they were knocked out by this band named Oasis with a song called 'Some Might Say,'" she recalls. "I knew a little bit of rock music, but I listened to that, and I was like, 'What the hell is this? This doesn't sound like Bon Jovi.' And the song was catchy. The other thing is that I knew enough English, but it was still not my first language, and though Liam and Noel now are sometimes difficult to understand when they talk, when they sing, at least to my non-native English ear, the words are very, very clear. So I could listen to the song one time, and I would know exactly what they were saying."

The music also gave Rasha a secret: she preferred the guitars and rock to the boy band pop her friends still loved. She next heard "Roll with It," and started paying attention whenever Oasis had a new song. Then tween tragedy struck: "The TV decided to stop. They stopped showing the top fifty. So I never saw another video until much, much later," she says. Still, she listened where she could. "We had antennas on our TV and we would sometimes pick up some of the signals from Syria, and Syria had more Western songs, Western music and shows and programs," she says, which is how she finally saw the "Wonderwall" video, and eventually others as well. "I heard 'D'You Know What I Mean?' in '97. The lyrics really resonated, because it was a rough time being a teenager growing up under sanctions in Iraq. Also, it wasn't full-blown war, but the U.S., from time to time, would bomb us, so it wasn't always peaceful," she remembers. "What I loved about 'D'You Know What I Mean?' is it sounded like, 'Look, it's rough, it's not easy, but you're gonna get through this. And this is life. You have one chance to live it, don't waste it on moping.' That's what Oasis sound like to me. And I think that's the best antidepressant. Because if you allow yourself to wallow too much in misery, I don't think there's a good outcome to that. And music was my escape for a long time. I think it was the only thing. The radio was the only thing I had going on. I learned to love that type of music. I learned to love them very much. Oasis was like, 'Just believe it's okay and it will be okay.' They're also very hilarious. The few snippets I listened to on the radio, they always cracked me up, but I didn't have the opportunity to listen to a full album until 2003." That's when the internet made things a little more accessible, even in Iraq, and she could finally take a deep dive into the band she adored. "I loved everything I heard," she said. "I didn't necessarily enjoy *Definitely Maybe* more than I enjoyed *Standing on the Shoulder of Giants*. I love that one, too. It's almost like every song they have, every album." Still, there were some gaps in her knowledge that she eventually filled thanks to the internet: "I was not aware of the B-sides. I didn't hear all of them until after 2009, so it was kind of a treat."

Rasha, who now works as a political analyst, and grew up in a distinctly political environment, enjoyed a band that she saw as decidedly apolitical. "That was a breath of fresh air," she says. "I have friends who tell me, 'Oh, they've never spoke about Palestine.' But they represent the working class that, globally, cannot afford to actually think about foreign policy because they're too concerned with 'Okay, when is my next meal coming? How do I put food on the table?' I mean, we need to consider this is their audience and the few people from the working class in the U.K. that I've met are all also like this. They can't afford that liberal, wealthy, upper-class privilege of 'Oh, let's think about what's happening in the rest of the world.' I have no doubt that they're decent human beings, and they have a very lovely side, but artists not expressing political opinions is something I very much encourage. That was refreshing. I didn't care that they never spoke about the Middle East. But they spoke up when the sad terrorist attack happened in Manchester and when the Grenfell Tower tragedy happened. They had opinions on that. And that was more than enough."

Rasha left Iraq in 2013, and because Oasis never toured through Iraq, she never managed to see them live. When the reunion shows were announced she was determined. There was just one little problem: "The queue in the U.S. was on October 2, which was a Tuesday. That was my first day at my new job and we had to be in the office Tuesdays and Thursdays. The tickets were going on sale at two p.m., that's exactly when our meeting is and we have to all meet in a certain room," she says, laughing. "I brought my laptop, and I'm pretending to listen. I'm looking at the queue, sixteen thousand, then fourteen thousand, and I'm talking about militias, and I'm talking about, you know, Iranian influence in the region. And then I'm thinking, 'Okay, I'm three thousand,' and then I get the ticket, and I could no longer focus." Like many other fans, Rasha ran into technical difficulties and the seats she wanted kept disappearing. She finally managed to get two tickets, but she was still in the meeting and couldn't scream or jump or celebrate in anyway. She couldn't even tweet about it, which is a shame, as she loves to tweet, particularly at Liam. She has his responses to her printed out on her fridge. She will always appreciate the band for what they did for her: "They made a tough period a bit more tolerable."

———

Sarah Peck and Kenny Davis were watching Liam Gallagher play at Reading Festival in 2024 when something interesting happened—a date was displayed on the giant screen behind him: "27.08.24. 8am."

They thought it was going to be an announcement of some anniversary celebration for *(What's the Story) Morning Glory?* but they also hoped that maybe it was more. "We have been talking about this since we met ten years ago. 'Will they? Won't they?'" she says. "When we saw that flash up on the screen, I was like, 'Oh, okay, this could finally be the moment that we've been waiting for.' So we were very excited." Sarah and Kenny are both huge Oasis fans and the band has played a pivotal role in their relationship.

Sarah and Kenny's first date was poignant, memorable and, according to Kenny, a little cringey. "This is embarrassing, but for our first date, we met at the Warwick Avenue station, which was right where Noel was living at the time in Little Venice—this was ten years ago—and we decided we were going to meet there and then have a walk past Noel's house, because that's what we both had in common from our teenage years." Both Sarah and Kenny had—separately—engaged in what seemed like a fairly common pastime for music-loving teens in Greater London in the nineties: go stand outside Liam's and Noel's houses and see if they appeared.

For Sarah it started when she was fifteen or so, when she found out that her favorite band in the world, Oasis, was recording their third album, *Be Here Now*, at Abbey Road Studios in London. She had one thought: "'Oh my gosh, this is my opportunity to go and meet Liam and Noel,'" she says. She and her friends left school, traveled about forty-five minutes on the train, and went to stand outside the studio. They were trying to confirm that Oasis was there when something miraculous happened. "Bonehead suddenly walked out of the house next door to Abbey Road, so he was obviously staying in that house," she says. "We started chatting to Bonehead, and we thought, 'Oh my god, we've met Bonehead! This is amazing, this is the most exciting thing ever.' And he told us that Liam wasn't in that day, but he said that Noel should be coming down to the studio. And I was looking at my friend, who was facing away from the Abbey Road crossing, and my friend's jaw just dropped in front of me, and I was like, 'Oh my gosh, okay.' I turned around, and I remember seeing Noel Gallagher midway across the famous Abbey Road Beatles crossing." Noel stopped and chatted with them and signed a few autographs before heading into the studio. For Sarah it was revelatory, not just because she got to meet the band, but because she realized that they were all living nearby.

After that, she and her friends made swinging by the Gallaghers' houses part of their routine. They were there one day when the press was gathered outside Liam's house. "It was the day that he got arrested for possession of cocaine or something like that," Sarah says, and Sky News asked her, at fifteen, for comment. They were also outside during Noel's thirtieth birthday, with Kate Moss and other celebrities walking in and out. The funny thing is, the Gallaghers didn't seem to mind the attention. "I think they were quite enjoying the fame, as it was all quite fresh to them back then," Sarah says. They would pop out and chat to the fans milling about outside, sign a few autographs, and then go about their day. Once the teens got their autographs, they would head off, too. "We weren't sitting there all day staring at their houses. We were quite respectful," says Sarah. "I wouldn't have done it if I thought they were uncomfortable with it. Their reactions back then were quite welcoming. The more and more famous they got, well, they can't really go anywhere now, but back in those days . . . "

Loitering around outside the houses made it easy to meet other

like-minded Oasis fans. After all, they were all there for the same reason. "It created this little Oasis community," Sarah says.

"There were quite a few other fans that we met outside, and some
of them are, like, my best friends today, still. It just became this thing,
every time we had a spare day, we would go up to Abbey Road and
walk around St. John's Wood and meet up with other Oasis fans, try
and see if we could catch a glimpse of Liam or Noel."

Sarah Peck getting an autograph

Kenny has a similar story. He and his friends came into London
from Newbury, an hour or so on the train, trying to find the Gallaghers' houses after having done some detective work using pictures of
their homes that were in the papers, an A to Z street map, and some
legwork. "We found out Liam lived near Primrose Hill, and the day
we went up, he wasn't in, but there were some guys there who said,
'Oh, we know where Noel lives,' and we said, 'Amazing, can we come

with you?' So we all walked over to Noel's house, Supernova Heights, but he wasn't in, either." Now that he knew where they both lived, he and his friends would come once a month or so just to see if the guys happened to be around.

"One of the first times I met Noel was on a Sunday morning. I think it was the thirty-first of August '97." He remembers the exact date because it was the day that Princess Diana died. He and his friend went to London, paid their respects at Kensington Palace, and then went around to see if the Gallaghers were home. Liam wasn't there, so they wandered to Noel's house and got lucky. "Noel popped his head around the corner," Kenny says. "I was definitely starstruck, but we started chatting about the news." Kenny had an Oasis calendar with him and was hoping to get it signed and handed it over to Noel. "And he looked at me and was like, 'You sure?' I was like, 'Yes, please. Yeah, sign it.' And he looked at the calendar again. He goes, 'Are you sure?' I looked at the calendar and saw that it was open to a picture of Liam, so I slowly changed it to a picture of Noel and he signed it."

Despite being in similar circles, Kenny and Sarah didn't meet until a website that matched people based on their musical taste brought them together. Kenny saw some of Sarah's photos, including one she snapped with Liam, and he reached out. They've been together ever since, sharing memories of the band, watching videos and concert footage, and collecting memorabilia. "Maybe if I hadn't had that experience outside of Liam's and Noel's houses and put those pictures up, maybe you and I would never have started talking," Sarah says. "Maybe not," says Kenny.

On the day that tickets for the reunion shows went on sale, they happened to be in Manchester. "We said, 'Let's go and get some good luck,'" says Sarah. They took themselves on an Oasis tour, including to Sifters Records in Burnage where the Gallaghers would shop, to Peggy Gallagher's house, and checked out all the new Oasis street art that had popped up when news of the reunion came out. The luck worked: they got tickets to Heaton Park, Wembley Stadium, and the Rose Bowl.

———

Toronto's premiere Oasis cover band, SuperSonic, has been playing together since Oasis split up, filling in a gap left by the Gallaghers. "We wanted to start a band, and we did some Oasis stuff, and I kind of sounded a little bit like Liam, and they said, 'Well, why don't we do a tribute?'" says Dylan Shepherd, lead singer, aka the Liam of Super-Sonic. "I've been doing it for, like, fifteen years now."

The band has brought their version of Oasis across North America, playing "Cigarettes & Alcohol" and "Live Forever" in Philadelphia, Edmonton, Chicago, New York, and West Hollywood. "We played at the Whisky on basically the thirtieth anniversary of them playing in L.A. at the Whisky," he says. "We were onstage when the clock struck midnight, and it was thirty years since they were onstage there." They also did a thirtieth-anniversary celebration of *Definitely Maybe*, where they played the band's '94 set list at the show. They strive for verisimilitude in their work. Dylan has even had the same haircut for fifteen years to cosplay as Liam. "I even grew it out one year to try and do, like, a bit of a Knebworth thing," he says, laughing. "We take painstaking efforts to emulate the band, the members of the band. For instance, the guy that does the Noel Gallagher in the band, he has the Union Jack Epiphone that Noel used. He's got the red 355 that he used later on in his career. He's got a black Les Paul that he used on the first tour in North America."

While some Oasis cover bands might have been concerned that they would have to stop playing now that Oasis is back, SuperSonic has found an uptick in gigs as excitement ramps up for the reunion shows, which they see as a sign of hope for the future. Another sign they look to is that audiences aren't just made up of Gen X and millennial fans. "What we've been seeing, probably for the last two years, is the audience is starting to get younger, and there's more young people who are actually getting into the band," Dylan says. "Last year, we did that *Definitely Maybe* thirty tour and the amount of young people that came out and, surprisingly, knew the songs intimately was pretty awesome." SuperSonic will have new source material to study when the entire band makes their way to Manchester to take their place among the audience at Oasis's reunion concert.

———

The first time Asis Patel heard Oasis was when his mum had finally been able to get a house of her own and move her two young sons out of her parents' house in Otley, outside Leeds, and into a council estate down the road. For Christmas the next year, the family got a stereo and a CD player to go with it. "She bought me *Definitely Maybe* and that was the first CD that was played on that stereo," Asis recalls. "Every time I hear *Definitely Maybe* I just come back to that thought. Just new beginnings, my mum buying the house, and getting the record and listening to it on the stereo for the first time that we got that Christmas." Asis thinks his mom bought him the album, because living in a small northern England town, she saw her little family reflected in it. "It was me and my brother and my mum, like Oasis was led by two brothers who grew up with their mum," he says.

Asis really fell for Oasis years later, when *Heathen Chemistry* came out in 2002. "That was the one that really got me, and that was the album that I really fell in love with," he says. "And then when I went to uni, that's when a good friend of mine, we bonded over Oasis in first year." Asis also started to play music and sing, thanks in large part to Oasis.

While Asis hasn't seen Oasis before, he did see Liam at Knebworth in June 2022 and saw Noel's High Flying Birds play at Glastonbury the same month. "So that's, like, my way of saying I saw Oasis," he says. He also saw Noel when he played on the beach in Brighton in 2023 and made him a card that he and all his friends signed to thank him for all the music he made. "We got the security guard to go backstage and give it to him, and he didn't come back with it, so I'm kind of telling myself that he got the card that we made for him," he says.

Asis did manage to get a ticket to the reunion show, after a friend got through the relentless queue. However, after he thought about it and weighed the cost, he ended up telling the friend to find someone else. "I couldn't justify paying three hundred and fifty pounds for it, as me being an artist, myself, also creating to earn a living," he says. "I actually went back to my mum's, and remembered what got me into Oasis in the first place. Growing up with my mum and brother, playing out as kids, and just being ourselves. And it made me think that the reunion feels like a business thing. It feels like they lost the soul of who they were, you know? I'm looking at the people who I grew up around and three hundred and fifty pounds, that's, like, rent for the month. The true fans of Oasis, they probably have, like, three, four kids to look after, and the fact that Oasis—who also came from that background—to have the nerve to actually charge their fans three hundred and fifty pounds per person, it just really upset me, and I thought, 'Nah, I can't.'"

————

Bernadette Gilbey, the California fan who travels extensively to see the band, wasn't entirely surprised that Oasis reunited. A little birdie had given her a hint when a friend who works at what she describes as the U.K.'s Live Nation equivalent tipped her off that something big was coming. "He wouldn't say who, but he says that people have been telling him it is a massive reunion tour and it's either Spice Girls or Oasis—and you obviously don't know me if you think I'm going to be interested in seeing a Spice Girls reunion," she says. "I held off on the news for a few days, and then told Tina [Snell]. I was like, 'Something's supposed to be announced Monday morning,' and I set my alarm, but I think the announcement didn't come at the time I thought it would, and so I just went back to sleep. Then I woke up that morning to a BBC alert that Oasis had reunited. And then Instagram and everything was just absolutely blowing up, so I was in my little bed in Long Beach, waking up to this news, and then instantly jumping around my apartment.

"The excitement was mostly about that I had seen them so many times, but I knew so many people that were too young—some of the current fans had not been born—that have never seen them," she continues. "And I was more excited they're going to be able to experience this. I knew it was not going to be the same magic as the original lineup, but I was happy to be able to share this experience with all of these people that I had met since the band broke up in 2009, and we're all going to be able to go and do this together. And part of it, too, is 'Okay, people, you can stop bitching about not seeing Oasis because now you've seen them.'"

————

The next generation of fans are excited to see the band. The first night of the Oasis reunion tour is set for July 4 at the Principality Stadium in Cardiff, Wales. If all goes according to plan, Grace Newman will be in the audience when Oasis takes the stage for the second night at the stadium. It will be fifteen-year-old Grace's first-ever concert.

Grace earned her fandom the old-fashioned way—by being forced to listen to the band by her parents. "My mum, she literally just had it on in the car constantly. My brother's also a fan as well," she explains with a laugh. While she admittedly hated her mother's musical obsession for a while, she now ardently loves the band. "Now Oasis is at the top of both of our Spotify Wrapped," she says.

Her mom, Tamara Newman, jumps in to add that Grace really is a fan. "She read the book *Supersonic*, and she got in touch with— I don't know how she got in touch with them—but she got in touch with Sawmills, which is where they recorded *Definitely Maybe*. It's a recording studio down in Cornwall. We happened to be going to Cornwall, so she messaged the owners and said, 'Could I have a photograph taken outside?' And they said, 'Well, not really, because we're on water.' It was an island," Newman says, laughing. While a photo wasn't possible due to those geographic reasons, the owners of Sawmills offered to give the family a tour of the facility. "As with so many people now, money's tight, so we didn't quite know what to do," says Newman. "They said that they'd give us a tour, but I had to tell her, it's going to depend on how much it costs." Grace reached back out and the son of the owner of Sawmills said he'd do it for free. "That isn't the kind of thing that happens to people like us, you know? We're just down-to-earth, hardworking people," says Newman. "So we went down to a place called Fowey and he came over on his boat, which was quite old. How would you describe the boat, Grace?"

"Old."

"Right. It was a little old jet boat, and he took us over to Sawmills and gave us a personal tour. We got to see the recording studios and hear about the other bands that have recorded there as well. The band Supergrass recorded there. They've got some equipment from Abbey Road, which would have been the Beatles', and it was just a phenomenal tour. And he's such a lovely chap. And then he took us back to the mainland, and it was just amazing."

Thanks to the tour, Grace was able to get the photo she wanted, and it turned out even better than she had hoped. "I got a photo of the ocean and stuff," Grace says. "I just took the photo, and then later on, I looked at the photos of Oasis there, and I compared the two photos, and I got the exact same angle as one of the Noel, Liam, and Bonehead, I think, where they stood in front of it, and it's just the exact same thing there!"

That's why they were so excited when they managed to get two tickets to the reunion show in Cardiff. Tamara wasn't planning on going, though. "I said to my daughter, she'd probably be better to go with my husband, because it's going to be really busy, and since COVID I've had quite bad anxiety," she explains. "But every time

Grace Newman on her tour of Sawmills Studio

they talked about it, I sulked. So my husband's now going to have to go and sit in a car in Cardiff for eight to ten hours."

It seems likely that both Tamara and Grace will be in tears at the show. "I think literally any song could play and I would be so excited," Grace says. "I think Liam Gallagher could literally go up and, like, swear at everyone onstage and then leave, and I'd probably be crying out of happiness just to be there."

Tamara seems to feel exactly the same way, but she does have a longer and more poignant history with Oasis. The band was the soundtrack to some difficult moments. "Back in the nineties I had a beaten-up VW Beetle, and I used to listen to Oasis all the time on my old tape deck and the CD player. I was pregnant at the time and I broke down on part of a motorway. I had to push the car on my own because nobody stopped to help me, being pregnant in the rain, with my old VW Beetle, waiting for somebody to come and help me. I just sat in my car crying, listening to Oasis," she says. That experience didn't turn her off the band or even her beloved *Definitely Maybe*. The band and album have been her constant companions since the early nineties, helping her manage a challenging childhood. "My mum passed away when I was ten, and I was adopted. I'm half Malay, and back in the seventies, people weren't as kind about race as they are now, so I just had a really bad time at school," Tamara says, explaining that eventually the music of Oasis helped her cope with it all. Despite burning through cassettes and CDs of the band's music, she never got to see them live, because the band never played nearby ("We live in a small area at the very bottom of the U.K., and it's not anywhere that anybody comes"), and she simply didn't have the money or means to travel to see them. "So to be able to take my daughter to see them is lovely," Tamara says, her voice cracking. Here she hands the phone to Grace, because she can't talk anymore. "It's very sad to see her cry, but it also does make me very excited for her to be able to go and see them," Grace says. "She's been a fan for thirty years, and she can finally see them."

---

When the tour rolls into Soldier Field in Chicago, Taylor Roebuck and her twin sister, Olivia, will be in the audience wearing the Oasis T-shirts they got for Christmas when they were eleven years old.

Taylor, who is the lead singer of the band Smut, has been a fan of Oasis since middle school, when her dad sat her and her two sisters down to listen to "Champagne Supernova" on the desktop computer in the family den around 2005. "Being like a couple of eleven-year-olds, we just kind of made fun of their haircuts the whole time," Taylor says from her home in Chicago. "But then the music sort of stuck. Of course, we didn't want to admit that our *dad* had put us on to something that we actually liked, but we started looking them up on our own on YouTube. We just watched all the music videos. By the time Christmas rolled around, we had like a full-on Oasis-themed Christmas. Like, every gift we had was a poster or a CD or a pin or a bag. Any memorabilia or merchandise my parents could find on eBay was wrapped up. That was the entire holiday."

Her love of Oasis didn't just manifest in a sweet collection of swag, but also in a love of music that eventually led to being in a band. Perhaps more important, though, Oasis made her feel like she *could* be in one. "To me, music seemed like this massive thing that's really difficult to understand, and it felt like you had to be some kind of a genius, but in all these interviews, the Gallaghers were so self-assured and confident and with this we-just-did-it attitude. They just presented themselves as rock stars kind of from the get-go," Taylor explains. "Around that time, I was writing a lot—we hadn't formed the band yet—but I started writing around that time because I was like, 'Maybe you can just do it?' I don't know if it was cockiness or confidence, but I was like, 'What if I am good enough? What if the secret to it is just assuming that it's easy and that you're really cool and talented and then it'll just happen for you?' I feel like I kind of use that as an ethos. It's almost a fake-it-till-you-make-it thing, and it was all because of Oasis."

Also attending the Soldier Field show is Smut's drummer, Aidan O'Connor, who became an Oasis fan while attending college, starting in 2017. "I had a roommate who, funnily enough, was a card-carrying Weezer Fan Club member, number, like, sixty or something, but he would just watch Oasis music videos and live clips until the wee hours of the morning, like every morning. We would just sit there, and we'd just be transfixed by Liam's charisma and listening to Noel's commentary on everything, his cynical kind of takes on everything. It was just very entertaining. After class, we would just meet in his room— an eight-by-eight room with one of those cheap fifty-inch TVs—and we'd sit down and watch music videos all day, and we would just blast the stereo. And, you know, those were great formative music-listening years for me."

Being a fan who came in to the fandom later meant playing a little bit of catch-up. "I think that the rivalry and the tabloids and just the, for lack of a better word, the lore about the band, the mythology of it all, felt very distant," says O'Connor. Hours of watching old concert footage and YouTube compilations helped him learn everything they could about the band. "I've loved going back, digging into these videos online, like the ones on the evolution of Liam Gallagher's voice. I just kept digging. I just kept digging down and staying hungry for all those little shreds of information that I could grab on to."

Through the fan community and music back channels, O'Connor and Roebuck had heard rumors that Oasis might be reuniting, but they didn't want to get their hopes up too high. "Only after it was officially announced, then I let myself become excited," says O'Connor.

"We were recording our album in New York when the tickets went on sale," O'Connor says. "So in between takes, we're, like, checking our phones on the wait list. It was really a crazy energy in the room because we were already doing our project, and then all of a sudden, boom, we have to buy these two-hundred-dollar tickets, like immediately, as soon as possible. Lots of different emotions in that week for sure."

———

A tiny storefront on one of Manchester's busy commercial bystreets is a mandatory stop for Oasis fans. It's the home of Microdot Boutique, the workshop of Brian Cannon, the designer who is indelibly intertwined with Oasis. It was Cannon who designed the now-famous Oasis box logo seen on shirts and albums. He also designed the album sleeves for *Definitely Maybe* and *(What's the Story) Morning Glory?*, working with photographer Michael Spencer Jones to create those memorable covers. The storefront on King Street is filled with prints of those photos as well as other assorted Oasis memorabilia. Twenty-four-year-old employee Frank Oldham is patiently telling eager customers about the Oasis prints on the walls and the blue fireplace that was in Bonehead's house and memorialized on the *Definitely Maybe* album cover. Oldham knows his stuff, not just because he's a diligent employee, but because he's been a fan of Oasis since he discovered their music as a teen, several years after the band had broken up. "I'm from a working-class family in Nottingham and there was something very relatable about them; even I couldn't quite put my finger on it as a teenager," he explains. "It just felt like lads that I would have hung around with or would have been pals with, you know? And then them singing such passionate music. They are normal, everyday people, who by the sound of it have gone through similar experiences to a lot of the lads from working-class backgrounds. And I think that's really what resonates about them is they feel like everyday people, you know? You meet these kind of characters at school, at the pub, at work, and they're up there on the big stage singing to hundreds of thousands of people. There's something definitely relatable and sincere about it, I suppose, and that's something that pulled me in for sure."

It was Oasis, in part, that inspired Oldham to become a musician and songwriter, too, performing under the name Frank & the Beats. "As a songwriter Noel couldn't do anything wrong in the early nineties," says Oldham, who had not yet born. "You have this perfect blend of high energy and then reflection as well. I'm not sure we'll ever have a band like that again."

While Oldham, like many other fans, faced technical difficulties while trying to secure tickets to the reunion gigs, he is going to see the band for the first time at their show in Manchester. "I mean, to see them in their own city, it's going to be a special night," he says. The one thing he is probably not going to do is buy a T-shirt, though. "I mean, it depends what they've got available at the gig, you know?" he says. "But if they've got the same stuff as they've got at Microdot and I can make use of my staff discount, why not buy it here?"

———

Whenever Liam Snell wants to impress his friends, he tells them one fact: his dad opened for Oasis at JC Dobbs in Philadelphia in 1994. Of course, that particular bit of bragging works better when your friends actually know who Oasis is. "That is the one thing I am working on. I'm trying to get my friends into Oasis," he says.

Despite the fact that his friends don't have strong opinions on Oasis B-sides, the sixteen-year-old is a big fan. So big that, for his birthday, his dad got them tickets to see the reunion show when the band comes to New Jersey, near where his father saw them play at Maxwell's in the nineties.

Liam remembers first hearing the band when he was around eleven or twelve. "I was just in the car with my dad and I remember this awesome guitar noise coming on and I was like, 'Wow, that is just so incredibly powerful. There's nothing like it.'" It was "Supersonic," and he immediately asked his dad to play more. Soon he was listening on his own, watching the *Supersonic* documentary and learning to play their songs on guitar, specifically on a Union Jack–emblazoned one like Noel's. "I can play quite a few Oasis songs," he says. "I can play all of *Definitely Maybe*, including the B-sides."

For Liam, whose name was inspired by the Gallaghers, he just

Liam Snell playing his own Union Jack

likes what he hears. "I think it's the fact that Liam and Noel are brothers, and that they have this special chemistry," he says. "Noel can just write these amazing songs using two or three chords, and just blows me away every time. 'Live Forever' is written using, I think, four chords, and it's one of the greatest songs I've ever heard."

For his dad, it's been fun to experience the band again. He never wanted to force his kids to listen to the music he liked, but has been thrilled to see it develop on its own. "I still love them as much now as I did then," says Jason. "It's just awesome that he has grasped onto the magic and has taken such a liking to it. It's really cool."

---

"To have an Oasis reunion, I can't explain what that felt like as a fan. It's something that I never thought that I would ever get to experience. I hoped that I would, but realistically, I didn't think there was really much of a chance of it," says Emma Arenstarr. The twenty-year-old from Dorset, England, first fell in love with Oasis when she watched the "Don't Look Back in Anger" video. The band became an obsession, but one with a bit of a cost in that it alienated her from her friends. "While growing up, nobody, like none of my friends, liked the same stuff as me," she says. "They were very much into whatever was hot at the time. And I've always loved older music." Specifically, she loved the music of Oasis and their attitude. "They do what they like and they just don't care," Emma says.

Like many of the fans who came before her, Emma found a connection in their music and a community in their fan base. "I was often bullied," she says. "Being bullied, it does take away from your confidence a lot. And, you know, finding Oasis really helped with that. It helped rebuild my confidence. And now I have loads of friends that I've met through various forums or fan sites or whatever who do love the same things as me, and it's, I just find it amazing how music can do that, you know, because I've got friends that are from the U.K., like me. And then I've got friends who are in America or Japan, and the fact that, you know, through a band you can meet people from all over the world is just incredible."

Not only has Emma found a group of like-minded friends online, but she's also spoken to her idol Liam Gallagher quite regularly on Twitter, aka X. "It's such a rare thing for artists to have that much of a connection with their fans," she says. "Getting to say that I speak to Liam on Twitter is, it feels like a complete dream, to be honest."

Emma did manage to get tickets to see Oasis when they play at Wembley Stadium. "It hasn't sunk in yet, to be honest. I don't think it will sink in until I'm in the stadium. And when I see them there, because at the moment I still can't believe it," she says. "To have Oasis back, you know, it's what the world really needs, is some good rock and roll."

———

The opening night of the reunion tour in Cardiff will be the first big concert for eleven-year-old River Cunningham. His dad, Ian, is a big fan of the band, but like his son, he has also never seen Oasis in concert. At thirty-three years old, the musician and music industry plant had sort of missed the band during their heyday. "It was one of those bands for me that was never going to get back together, you know? I put them up there with the Smiths and the Talking Heads; if you missed it, it's too late kind of a thing," Ian says. That all changed when Oasis announced the reunion. "They first announced the European dates, but they hadn't announced any in the U.S. yet," he says. "Possible U.S. tour dates were leaking in screenshots on Twitter, but it wasn't confirmed. Since I wasn't actually sure if I was going to be able to get tickets to the U.S., I figured I should just go for it. Also, what better way to see Oasis for the first time than in the U.K.? And then I was like, 'Well, if I'm going to go see Oasis this summer, I have to take my kid.' I don't even know how many Oasis songs he knows, other than the ones I've played him, but he's old enough at eleven that it's going to be something he'll remember. And it's one of those shows that when he's thirtysomething, he can go, 'Yeah, I saw them back in the day.'" So Ian made a plan: get tickets, get the kid a passport, then get the kid to Wales for his first international trip. While not entirely sure what to expect from the concert or the travel, River explains that he's "really, really, really excited." With that attitude among kids these days, it seems clear that Oasis will have fans for years and generations to come.

# WHATEVER

As this is being written, Oasis reunion shows from Cardiff to Korea, Argentina to Canada, London to Los Angeles have all sold out. The band is back together. Liam and Noel Gallagher figured out a way to make a yearslong rift a thing of the past, proving once again that with any great story, the end is never truly the end. There can always be a sequel.

The Oasis reunion has opened another chapter for the band—one that feels like the beginning of something new both for the people onstage and for the fans gathered in front of it. When the Gallagher brothers once again pick up a guitar and take the mic, their return will be about more than nostalgia for Britpop or any other bygone era. For fans, this long-awaited return is a chance not only to relive the anthems that defined a generation, but to share the experience of hearing the first few notes of "Hello" or "Supersonic" blast out of the amps or the thrill of seeing Liam grab the mic and Noel hit his first few notes on "Slide Away." It's a chance for longtime devotees to share the power of live music with their spouses or kids and the opportunity for a whole generation of fans who never got to see Oasis perform live, either because of age or money or access, to sing along to "Wonderwall."

Fans who grew up listening to Oasis on their car radios or on cassette decks in their bedroom or in their parents' streaming library found music that spoke to them and has continued to speak to them for years. Many also found an origin story they could relate to and aspire to, hoping that they could follow in the footsteps of these two brothers from Burnage who rose up from their working-class roots on the strength of their incredible musical gifts, propelled forward by their enormous dreams.

The energy, excitement, tension, and talent onstage have been written about extensively. Hopefully the stories shared in this book make it clear that what was happening in front of the stage, up in the cheap seats, in ticket lines and parking lots and train stations, and alone in cars driving down quiet roads late at night was equally full of drama and dreams and people yearning for connection.

While the band is now back together, the fans have always been there, and they are the ones making sure that the story and sound of Oasis live forever.

# ACKNOWLEDGMENTS

This book sprouted from the idea that, at this point, everyone knows about Oasis, but no one has really talked about the fans. Personally, I find the people who camp out for tickets and sleep in train stations after shows, and spend their years and money traveling the world to hear the songs they love, so much more interesting. My agent suggested I write up a bite-sized pitch about it and then, somehow, miraculously, everyone at Gallery Books seemed to like the idea. A few months later this book was born, but it couldn't have been done without a huge support system.

Thanks to Oliver Benavidez for sparing me for a few weeks, and to Brian Benavidez for holding down all the forts to give me the time and space to write. Thanks to Stepfanie Aguilar and Jak Hutchcraft for all the research help and tracking down fans all over the world. I honestly couldn't have done it without you both. Thanks to Daniel Ralston and Nick Dawson for sharing ideas and contacts, and being generally great humans. Appreciate all the late-night texts, early-morning video calls, and widespread emotional support from Stefan Boublil, Gina Alvarez,

Michele Monteforte, Natasha Chetiyawardana, Maureen Yoshizaki, Grace Kim, Selena Castellanos, Eve Harlow, Rhiannon Ellis, A. J. D'Agostino, Jason Reitman, Nicole Spector, Courtney Smith, Niko Stratis, Josh Isaacs, Veronica Martin, Tami Taylor, Robert Smith, and Simon Le Bon. Thank you all for thinking I could pull this off.

Extra thanks to Dad and Esther for checking in on me all the time, to Kerry Donahue and Guy Story for a space to work, and to John Lambremont, Corina Kinnear, Zamari, and Allison Kave for keeping me sane while I frantically typed. As always, thanks to Jesse and Mark Locker and the rest of my family for tolerating me, checking in on me, and then leaving me alone so I could finish this book. Extra thanks to Debbie Ball, Eric Speck, Kyle Dale, Ken Weinstein, the fine folks at Pitch Perfect PR, and Rob Fiddaman for being incredible resources, and to Debbie Ellis, Brian Garcia, Tina Snell, and Jake McCarthy for sharing so much. Hat tip to Jonathan G. Schofield and Arielle Castillo for being excellent Manchester tour guides. Appreciate all the work by Debbie Kung, Ian Cunningham, and Nick Harmer to keep me in all the latest memes.

Huge thanks to my agent Lisa Gallagher, my backup agent, Shawn Dailey, and to Deryck Whibley for giving me a shot. Massive appreciation for Rebecca Strobel and Jennifer Bergstrom at Gallery Books for believing in this project from the first clink of a cocktail glass. Additional thanks to Aimée Bell, Sally Marvin, Lucy Nalen, John Paul Jones, Caroline Pallotta, Taylor Rondestvedt, and everyone at Gallery Books who helped make this feat possible.

Mostly, though, thank you to the many fans who shared their stories. This is your book.

# ABOUT THE AUTHOR

**Melissa Locker** is a writer, producer, podcaster, and on-air personality. Her music reporting has appeared in *The Guardian, Rolling Stone, Vanity Fair, Time, The Believer, Elle, Vogue, Pitchfork, Stereogum*, and beloved alt-weeklies including *The Village Voice*, the *Washington [D.C.] City Paper, The Stranger*, and the *Portland Mercury*. She has worked at New York's public radio station, WNYC; for the television show *Portlandia*; appeared in documentaries about Ace of Base and the Replacements; and worked at the legendary indie label Kill Rock Stars. Her music podcast company, Nevermind Media, tells music stories, including an oral history of the Blues Brothers and *The True Story of the Fake Zombies*. In addition to putting words on the page, she was an on-air culture reporter for the National Public Radio show *The Takeaway*.